ID0908708

International Federation of Library Associations and Institutions
Fédération Internationale des Associations de Bibliothécaires et des Bibliothèques
Internationaler Verband der bibliothekarischen Vereine und Institutionen
Международная Федерация Библиотечных Ассоциаций и Учреждений
Federación Internacional de Asociaciones de Bibliotecarios y Bibliotecas

IFLA Publications 64

Guidelines for
Legislative Libraries

Edited by Dermot Englefield

K·G·Saur
München · New Providence · London · Paris 1993

IFLA Publications
edited by Carol Henry

Guidelines for Legislative Libraries
Ed. by Dermot Englefield, for the Parliamentary
Libraries Sections of the International Federation
of Library Associations and Institutions
XV, 123 p., 21 cm
   (IFLA Publications; 64)
   ISBN 3-598-21792-7

Die Deutsche Bibliothek – CIP-Einheitsaufnahme

Guidelines for legislative libraries / ed. by Dermot Englefield,
for the Parliamentary Libraries Sections of the IFLA. –
München ; New Providence ; London ; Paris : Saur, 1993
   (IFLA publications ; 64)
   ISBN 3-598-21792-7
NE: Englefield, Dermot [Hrsg.]; International Federation of Library
Associations ans Institutions: IFLA publications

Printed on acid-free paper
The paper used in this publication meets the minimum requirements of American National
Standard for Information Sciences – Permanence of Paper for Printed Library Materials,
ANSI Z39.48-1984.

Druck / Printed by Strauss Offsetdruck GmbH, Hirschberg
Binden / Bound by Buchbinderei Schaumann, Darmstadt

ISBN 3-598-21792-7
ISSN 0344-6891 (IFLA Publications)

CONTENTS

PREFACE

FOREWORD
Dr Ernst Kohl, Bundestag, Bonn Germany

INTRODUCTION
Dermot Englefield

PART I
Roles and Framework
Dermot Englefield

PART II
Reference Services
Jane Ann Lindley

PART III
Research Services
William Robinson
Penelope Fay Heavner [Chapter 8]
with introductions by Jane Ann Lindley

PART IV
Special Services for Legislators
Brit Floistad, Jane Ann Lindley, Aileen Walker

A Note on the Contributors

PREFACE

The idea for this book came to the editor in 1987 when **IFLA** met in Brighton in the United Kingdom. At the time I was Chairman of the Parliamentary Libraries Section of IFLA and it struck me that information work for legislatures was not only growing and becoming more sophisticated in the case of developed democracies, but was also spreading to many areas of the world where strong legislatures had hardly been a glimmer in anybody's eye for decades. Since 1987, as the result of many revolutions in different parts of the world, the pace of change in this regard has speeded up still further.

I first discussed the question of a short monograph _Guidelines for Legislative Libraries_ in the Grand Hotel, Brighton, with Jane Ann Lindley of the Asia Foundation and formerly of the Congressional Research Service in Washington DC. She agreed to join the project and this was to prove important in view of the experience she was building up helping many Asian Parliamentary Libraries first while based in Islamabad in Pakistan and subsequently in Bangladesh. At the IFLA meeting in Moscow in 1991, William Robinson, Deputy Director of the Congressional Research Service and Brit Floisted, Librarian of the Norwegian Parliament in Oslo, joined the project. Subsequently, my own colleague Aileen Walker, who is responsible for the computer-based indexing of parliamentary papers and proceedings at Westminster, joined the team. Throughout the period 1989-1993 the support and encouragement of the present Chairman of the IFLA Parliamentary Libraries Section, Dr Ernst Kohl of the Bundestag, Bonn, Germany has been most welcome.

I am conscious that the writing of this book has taken much longer than was originally intended, but that, during this period, the whole scene with regard to legislatures and the information they need has altered. Maybe the book's protracted preparation has helped contributors, in judging a changing scene, to make the volume more useful for the future.

Guidelines for Legislative Libraries has been written not only for the Library profession as a whole, including those who are training, but also for those engaged in parliamentary librarianship and, in particular, for those involved in setting up new information services for legislators. This includes administrators and those who have responsibility for authorising funds for this purpose. The collecting, analysis and dissemination of information is expensive; lack of information, especially for those representing national opinion on an amazingly wide range of domestic and international issues, is even more expensive. It is important therefore that all concerned with providing services for legislators, including Members themselves, should understand these needs and the most effective method of establishing necessary support.

This is my last contribution to the work of **IFLA**. Since the meeting held in Budapest, over twenty years ago, I have been a willing participant at almost all of its annual meetings. I have learnt a great deal, had my ideas challenged and broadened and made a great number of friends. While thanking those who have been fellow contributors to this volume, I couple that appreciation with thanks to my **IFLA** friends for their support and kindness through the years and I wish them well in the future.

Dermot Englefield

Librarian
House of Commons
Westminster, United Kingdom

FOREWORD

"The practical choice of first-rate nations", writes Walter Bagehot in the introduction to the second edition of his political classic, *The English Constitution,* first published in 1867, "is between the Presidential government and the Parliamentary; no State can be first-rate which has not a government by discussion, and those are the only two existing species of that government. It is between them that a nation which has to choose its government must choose". The wave of democratization throughout the world which is a marked characteristic of the history of the last decade of the nineteenth century signals that people everywhere have become emancipated to make their "first-rate" choice now.

No one should be mistaken, however; representative government is the most difficult form of government, and it can be maintained that the decisive factor for its operational success in contemporary society is information. The average parliamentarian, as a rule, needs briefing and analytic support in order to be able to make informed political judgments or choices on usually difficult and complex issues, for otherwise the consequences of a political decision would become incalculable, and the representative system would ultimately discredit itself.

The primary agent for the provision of information on facts and events, and the latest results of academic research on the one hand, as well as on personalities, people's opinions and ideas on the other is the parliamentary library. The sustainability of the representative system to some extent, therefore, depends also on whether parliamentary libraries recognize and fulfill their specific mission successfully. This kind of information work, which distinguishes parliamentary libraries from other types of research libraries is however, rarely taught at library schools. That is why the *Guidelines for Legislative Libraries* is a most timely publication in the present political situation.

Ever since its establishment as a separate Section of the International Federation of Library Associations and Institutions (IFLA) in 1976, the Section of Parliamentary Libraries has tried to advance the professionalism of parliamentary librarians. At its open meetings during the annual IFLA General Conferences it has always attempted to include at least one paper on technical innovations in libraries, particularly automation, and often papers on organizational aspects of parliamentary library work. Since 1987, when IFLA introduced workshops as a specific type of gathering during the general conference, the Section of Parliamentary Libraries, together with the parliament of the host countries of the IFLA Conferences, has regularly organized full-day workshops in the host parliaments dedicated to an in-depth study of their particular library and information services. In addition, the Section has held a number of pre-conference seminars over the years dedicated to survey the state-of-the-art of parliamentary librarianship in a particular geographical region.

Some of the contributions to these *Guidelines for Legislative Libraries* have emanated from papers submitted to one or another of these conferences. With the Guidelines, the Section of Parliamentary Libraries has for the first time aimed at presenting a systematic approach to the various fields of activity of parliamentary librarianship. This book will, therefore, be indispensable to all who either work in, or are supervising, a parliamentary library, in particular in countries in the process of democratization. The contributors are all experienced parliamentary librarians. The editor (and also author of a number of chapters) Dermot Englefield, the Librarian of the House of Commons and a former Chairman of the Section of Parliamentary Libraries, can also draw on the sum total of his long professional experience. He will be retiring in the very year that the first edition of the Guidelines will be published. With this book he adds still another service to the many services which he has rendered to the worldwide community of parliamentary librarians. On behalf of the international Section of Parliamentary Libraries, I wholeheartedly acknowledge our debt of gratitude.

Ernst Kohl
Chairman
Section of Parliamentary Libraries
January 1993

INTRODUCTION

Guidelines for Legislative Libraries might have been called Guidelines for Parliamentary Libraries not least because it represents the work and views of members of the Parliamentary Libraries Section of **IFLA**. But in our discussions within the Section there have been awkward moments when representatives of Congresses, Diets, Assemblies, etc, have speculated that the word Parliament may be a little limited on the world stage, but that these representative bodies which they serve are normally required - among many other duties - to legislate; hence the title of this volume.

The libraries of legislatures are institutions that by the simplest of definitions are special libraries. They serve a particular and defined clientèle, namely the Member of the legislature, together with, increasingly, the Member's personal staff. Additionally they usually support the institution as a whole and sometimes play a curatorial role with regard to its archives.

But if you were designing a legislature from scratch, I am not sure that you would necessarily suggest it should have a library at all. The word **library** is lucidly defined in the Oxford English Dictionary as: "A place set apart to contain books for reading, study or reference". Somehow that does not ring true as being a description of the needs of a modern legislature. There is an overtone in the definition suggesting rows of leather-bound volumes, written by hallowed humanists setting out syntheses of earlier civilisations. The telephone, the fax and the photocopier are absent. And there is, in the definition, a total emphasis on books which increasingly are too out-of-date to match the tempo and currency of the needs of Members. The instant comment by a Member demanded by the media at an airport or a press conference; the wish to prove your political antagonist is out-of-date with his statistics; the need to use public debate often under the arc lights of a television studio, to wrong-foot your opposition: these all demand accuracy but also currency too great for the stately pace of book publishing. And so some of those shelves must become more flexible, with boxes of pamphlets, press notices and cuttings, official papers, proceedings of congresses and seminars (increasingly desk-top published), and videos. Some of these media are the subject of Chapter 11. Information on microfilm, more recently on CD-Rom and of course available from 'on-line' databases challenge those rows of handsome volumes not only in terms of currency, but also with demands for precious accommodation. Maybe what legislatures really need is not so much libraries as Information Centres which may grow to having Research Centres as well.

At Westminster there has been recently an alteration in the House of Commons Committee system which reflects this change of need and hence of terminology. Since 1818, when the House of Commons Library was founded, there has been for much of the time a Library Committee made up of Members of Parliament to represent their needs and views. For the last thirty years it has been a sub-committee of the House of Commons Services Committee. As a result of reorganisation in 1991, this watchdog became a full Select Committee with the title **'The Information Committee'** drawing together the Library, research and computer services run by and for the House of Commons. The establishment of this new major House of Commons Committee seems to me timely preparation for the information needs of the twenty-first century.

If you accept the need to update the idea of these support services for legislators, then you need to consider not only the sources which must be available but also the staff to exploit them on Members' behalf. The 1946 House of Commons Library had just six staff to watch over those handsome volumes, receive and register the papers and proceedings of Parliament and answer Members' reference enquiries. Today it has about 170 staff including economists, statisticians, lawyers, scientists and other specialists who respond to incessant questioning by Members. Developments in other legislatures are not dissimilar although where the definition of the work of the legislative library has remained a traditional and rather curatorial one, then the information services have sometimes been attached to other parts of the legislature's administration.

Guidelines for Legislative Libraries does not take a view on how library/research/information services should be organised within a particular legislature, other than to warn that these services are expensive, especially in terms of staff, and that therefore they need to be well coordinated in order to avoid duplication and waste.

There is one distinctive aspect of the work of these staff, when compared with the role of other staff of the legislature, which needs to be underlined. Most of the latter staff focus their work on what goes on in the building of the legislature itself. Proceedings in the Chamber and in Committees are the concern of procedural and committee staff: reporting debates are the concern of reporting staff: others are concerned with administration, security, accommodation, visitors, catering, etc, etc. But the staff concerned with library and information services by definition see the role of the Member in wide and well-rounded terms and always bear in mind that their information must match the Member's needs wherever he is working as a legislator. It may be, for instance, that his work representing his electorate is an important area where he is given support by the information staff who thereby learn some of the problems created by the laws passed by the legislature. Much of the information needed for Members comes, of course, from outside sources so staff must not only be very aware of changes in the outside world and its organisation but also be apt negotiators for help on behalf of Members. This external dimension also means that at the technical level the Library must keep up-to-date for fear some data ceases to be available in traditionally published form and has to be gathered through more up-to-date techniques, which of course normally render it more current.

Finally, information staff of legislatures can suffer from a certain professional isolation. Most countries have only one legislature and their staff have limited opportunities to discuss developments and exchange experiences with staff in other countries doing similar work. Federal countries will often have subordinate legislatures but in most cases these are staffed on a very small scale when compared with the national legislature (Australia, Canada and the United States are, to a degree, exceptions to this generalisation). This professional isolation has, in the last twenty years or so, been countered not only through the development of the work of the Parliamentary Libraries Section of **IFLA** but also by the growth of other organisations designed to link legislatures and to enable their staff to check developments in other Parliaments and indeed, if appropriate, to learn from the mistakes of others.

Most widespread, in that it covers parliaments throughout the world, is the work of the Information Centre of the Inter-Parliamentary Union in Geneva. Apart from being an interesting library of comparative information on legislatures, it runs technical programmes for the information staff of legislatures. A second institution was started in 1977 when member parliaments of the Council of Europe and the European Parliament set up the European Centre for Parliamentary Research and Documentation which built bridges first between the parliaments of Western European countries and more recently extended its remit to some of the Parliaments of Central and Eastern Europe. Cooperation between the Parliamentary Libraries in Australia took shape with the founding of the Association of Parliamentary Libraries of Australasia in the early 1970s. Papua New Guinea and New Zealand are members together with Australia itself and subsequently, Australia has taken up the broader role of becoming an umbrella organisation for those working in legislative information programmes in its part of the world. This was formulated following a Commonwealth Parliamentary Association meeting in Hobart in 1983, as the Parliamentary Libraries in the South-West Pacific project. In Canada the Association of Parliamentary Libraries was formed at a meeting in Toronto in 1975 and the same year in the United States the National Conference of State Legislatures was established and within it the Legislative Research Libraries Staff Section. Much older than any of these organisations is the Parliamentary Libraries of Nordic Countries. The first meeting of this organisation took place in 1922, which is five years before **IFLA** itself was founded. The countries include: Denmark, Finland, Iceland, Norway and Sweden. Most recently, and stimulated by the work of the Parliamentary Libraries Section of **IFLA** and by the **IFLA** Conference held in Tokyo in 1986, there has been established an organisation covering the Parliamentary Libraries of South-East Asia, which has had two very successful meetings. Discussions have been held in other areas of the world along these lines including East and Central Africa and certain countries in South America.

I catalogue these developments, mostly during the last twenty years or so, because they suggest a very real coming together of people and ideas concerned with offering and sustaining Library services for legislatures, and which are an integral part of supporting working democracy. These changes, together with the information needs in the new or reconstituted legislatures of many countries, form the background to the preparation of _Guidelines for Legislative Libraries_, a book which it is hoped will be of assistance to all those involved or aspiring to take part in this work.

Part 1 of the book discusses the broad context of legislative information services. Part 11 is concerned with the development of Reference Services which are the normal starting points of support for the legislature. Part 111 is the other end of the spectrum, namely an account of specialist research services on a grand scale, but it contains full discussion of the gradation of support for Members from reference to research services in depth. Part 1V discusses some particular aspects of services for legislatures including the information in the media, the role of the computer in general and an account of the latter's use in the ordering and analysis of the proceedings and papers of one parliament in particular.

There is no Conclusion because it would be wrong to close the door on the dynamic situation that information work for parliaments currently represents. It would also be wrong to finish with a blueprint for an ideal library. The study of parliaments in many parts of the world has convinced me that a country's political culture and all that goes with it is strongly indigenous so that *Guidelines for Legislative Libraries* is very much just a beginning. Each individual legislature and its library will have to decide how far it should go and by what route.

GUIDELINES FOR LEGISLATIVE LIBRARIES

PART I

ROLES AND FRAMEWORK

Introduction

The staff of legislative libraries are often conscious of living in two worlds – that of being an official of a legislature and that of being a librarian. Sometimes they may not be sure of which to set down as their profession in their passport. The truth is they are very active information brokers for a group of people (the legislature) who although they are skilful manipulators of information are seldom interested in how it is selected and collated. For the most part they want the answer not just the resources for the answer which involves the legislative library being a highly dynamic information service. In addition they need it to be absolutely up to date and absolutely accurate for fear they may be challenged especially in public. Their resources are minute compared with those of the government whose policy they may wish to question and this reflects itself in the challenge there is for those who follow the calling of legislative librarianship.

Part I of these Guidelines is concerned with the broad issues of the nature of the legislature, its need for information, the different administrative structures and some of the practical problems known to librarians but seen in the context of a legislature.

CHAPTER I

LEGISLATURE

1.01 The detailed role of the library of the legislature is to a considerable degree determined by whether a country is a federal or a unitary state. Federal states include Australia, Canada, India, Spain, the United States and West Germany. Unitary states would include Japan, Sweden and the United Kingdom.

1.02 The yardstick here is whether there is a power to legislate below national level. If so we are talking of a form of federal state and if a country is federated then to some degree there are two levels of legislating and thus for legislative libraries two levels of subject focus.

1.03 From the legislative library viewpoint however the level of <u>legislative responsibility</u> is not the only matter involved. There is also the fact that <u>responsibility for the administration of society</u> will in a federal state be at two levels. And this responsibility is obviously of great and specific interest to the legislator when representing his constituent. (Unitary state legislators have a similar problem in distinguishing between what might be seen as their responsibility and what is the responsibility of local government councillors).

1.04 If we are considering the legislature's library a checklist of its subject responsibilities needs to be made. The corollary of this is that in a federated country you will at the same time be preparing a checklist of subjects for the legislatures at a lower or provincial level.

1.05 In a unitary country it is inevitable that the work of the legislature and hence of its library will have to be at a greater level of detail and will also have to cover a wider range of subjects than in a federated country. It may also follow that a unitary country has a greater number of legislators than a federal country, eg the United States has 450 members of the House of Representatives for well over 200 million people and the United Kingdom 651 members of the House of Commons for less than 60 million people.

1.06 These factors may in turn have an impact on the level of specialisation needed in staffing both with regard to reference work and to research work if this is undertaken, and this in turn will help determine staffing policies. Naturally it similarly impacts on the legislative library's stock.

1.07 In determining the need for and the role of a legislative library it is vital therefore firstly to be clear concerning the actual role of the legislature itself.

CHAPTER 2

NATIONAL COMMUNICATIONS CONTEXT

2.01   The legislature is by definition an important part of the national communications network.   Its function includes gathering proposals from Government including proposals for legislation, securing information from Government and non–Government services, and listening to the views of constituents nation–wide through its Members' questions and comments in debates.   It both legislates for society and then checks on its administration.   Its proceedings and papers can have a wide distribution for further analysis and research or via the mediae for further public consumption.

2.02   Because of its position as a nodal point of current information, or for other historical reasons, the legislative library may have a very direct relationship with the national library.   In the US the national library developed from and remains called the Library of Congress.   In Japan, which is based on the US model, the National Diet Library is similar.   Both have had to develop a specific library and research service for the legislature within the national library.   In Canada and Australia the national libraries were separated from the legislature libraries in recent decades.   In most of the European countries the library of the legislatures are quite separate from the national libraries and always have been.   Finland is a special case in that the legislative library is the national library of the social sciences, which seems a logical way to organise matters in a small country.   In New Zealand it is only very recently that the legislature has decided to separate its legislative library from its national library.   The question of the relationship of the library of the legislature and the national library is an important one as it may impinge on matters of priority of service for Members, confidential information for Members and the whole question of national copyright for legislative libraries.   This latter point depends among other things on the scale of publishing in a country.   The libraries at Westminster for instance would never want a twentieth of the publications brought out in the UK.

2.03   The question of public access to the legislature's library will also depend on the latter's role as a national centre of research. Where possible most librarians seek to help bona fide students. However the staffs of many legislatures have expanded greatly in recent years and the library may have problems of accommodation for the public. Sometimes of course this expansion has led to new buildings which has solved these accommodation problems at least temporarily. As much information passing through the legislature is made public, it may be sufficient to restrict access only to sources not available elsewhere, but this will depend on the scale and accessibility of the nation's alternative sources. If the legislative library is responsible for the archives of the legislature then it does have the responsibility to ensure they are organised and available for research by members of the public.

2.04 The legislature's library may be given the remit to act as the clearing house of information for the public about the legislature's work. This may cover historical information as well as its current activities. This might include:

(a)   Regular bulletins on the legislature's work both past and proposed.

(b)   Summaries of its work each session, year or other longer period.

(c)   Short factsheets on different aspects of its work.

(d)   A service of information by telephone and letter.

(e)   Guides, especially to its documentation if there is a responsibility for archives.

(f)   If the legislature required, it might even include a form of Education Service for young people.

This service is likely to include among its users institutions like Government departments, firms of solicitors, the media etc, and also individual members of the public.

CHAPTER 3

INFORMATION AND THE LEGISLATURE

3.01   The staff supporting legislatures has in many cases grown greatly since World War II. How much support Members need is not an easy judgment and depends to some degree on how separate the legislature is from the executive (Government) and how independent it is. This in turn depends on the political culture of a country and its historical development and whether it has adopted any particular model for its political system.

Within the administration of the legislature itself the place of the library varies greatly. But its status within the organisation is quite fundamental to its development because it represents a judgment on its usefulness. That judgment may be made by administrators assigning resources between priorities, but it may also be made by Members themselves, who are the people who make use of the services (see 3.02 below). Most legislatures come under a presiding officer and are actually administered by a secretary–general. In this case the services for the legislature are centralised and the librarian would report either directly to the secretary general or, depending on the structure of the services, an official rather lower in the hierarchy. In some systems, especially where there is one library for a bicameral form of legislature (Australia and Canada) or a federated system of departments of supporting staff (House of Commons, Westminster) then the librarian may well report to the presiding officer himself. This reporting line obviously reflects the status of the library within the institution as a whole and the library is more effective and often efficient the higher up the hierarchy the librarian reports. Information services are very expensive and need to be husbanded and used effectively.

3.02   Because the legislative library is designed for Members its relationship with them is fundamental. The legislator is very exposed in his job and increasingly he acknowledges that it is a full–time one. He is under at least three growing pressures. The first is a demanding media which insists on his immediate reaction to policy

6

changes, crises and news – especially bad news. Secondly the society for which he has a stewardship is becoming ever more complicated and more technical. Thirdly with regard to news, time and space have been virtually eliminated and the reflex has in many cases replaced the considered response. All this change, and the catalogue could be extended, has resulted in the job of the legislator being a very high pressure one and very dependant on lucid and often brief exposition by Members. While this is an art that it might be expected politicians to possess, it does impinge on the role of the library itself. For instance Members need to be briefed very clearly, complex technical and legal issues need to be simplified and above all information, especially if it contains statistics, needs to be up-to-date. An argument based on out-of-date knowledge quickly turns into an embarrassment. Much the same can be said of accuracy, which is essential, especially when Members are in public debate or questioning not only in the legislature but also at press conferences, broadcasts, airport interviews etc.

A second factor in the relationship between the library and Members is the latter may not acknowledge any hierarchy between each other. They may all be sent to the legislature by groups of constituents and believe that the priority of their needs is as great as that of any other Member. Most institutions do not work on such a democratic principle and to do so can present problems to the staffs of legislatures.

Finally legislatures are highly charged institutions concerned with the clash of ideas and indeed of feelings among Members and the staff serving them need to appreciate this fact and respond accordingly.

3.03 The pressures mentioned above have, especially in recent years, resulted in the growth of Members' personal staff. The classic case is the US Congress where members of the House of Representatives may have nearly twenty staff and of the Senate nearly forty. But the legislators of some medium size countries have also started to be offered the option of one, two, sometimes three personal staff. From the library's point of view this can lead to a number of decisions having to be taken and possibly to a number of problems. An obvious first question is to what extent should

Members' personal staff be given access to the facilities really instituted for Members themselves? At the simplest level, should they be able to borrow material which Members may need or may wish to borrow themselves? Would it be possible to separate service to Members from service to their personal staff by offering the latter a form of branch library facility? Members' personal staff may well add a further link to the chain between the Member asking for information and the library staff providing it. This can quite easily be a recipe for misunderstanding, even confusion, and can lead to duplication and missed deadlines. Is all the information actually wanted by the Member and, if not, what control is there over the commissioning of work? And the obvious final question – to what extent does a Member's personal staff pass off as his work answers compiled by library staff? Not only may this hinder relations between the library staff and Members, but his personal staff member being naturally a non–specialist, may not really understand all the implications of the reply. As a simple example, this might happen with statistical information where the Member's personal staff is unaware of footnotes explaining changes in classification, baselines etc. In a public forum the Member might be subsequently embarrassed through questioning etc.

While Members may well feel that they need personal staff over whom they have complete control and who can add a necessary political dimension to their work, it is important that the information chain between provider and final user is kept as short and as clear as possible.

The final and the most important aspect of the relationship between library staff, indeed all legislature staff and Members and their personal staff, is that of political neutrality. Once again how easy or how difficult this matter is depends to a degree on the political culture of the country. The level of confidence between legislature staff and Member must be of the highest and this can only be achieved if all Members feel totally assured that there is no political bias in the information they and their fellow Members of all political persuasions are given. It is their job to add the political interpretation. Where this confidence in impartiality breaks down, as it did in the Australian Parliament at Canberra a few years ago, it can be damaging to everyone concerned.

3.04   The library does not only have this key relationship with Members and also with their personal staff, but in addition with other staff of the legislature and sometimes with the staff of political parties.

With regard to other legislature staff, as the total staff should add up to a cohesive and economic support service for the legislature, it is important that areas of responsibility are clearly defined and sustained. In the nature of human institutions this is not always entirely straightforward. For instance a legislature's relationship with the public needs to be cogently organised. It may range from that between Members and individuals or constituents which need not concern the staff of the legislature, through legislative committees and their chairmen, who may conduct their public relations with press conferences on their reports etc. to a legislative resource providing information for the public concerning Members, the legislature's work etc. Within the legislature, committees may wish to assemble specialist staff for a specific enquiry and, depending on its size and resources, the library may be called on to supply bibliographical or subject assistance. The committee may wish to combine assistance from their legislative staff with hiring the services of outside assistants who may be accepted national authorities in their fields. Whatever pattern of Member and/or committee support is chosen, it is vital that duties are undertaken in the most efficient way and that 'in-house' subject specialism of value including the library is well used. This is not only because the staff will know the tempo and temper of the legislature's work, but also because for the staff such research etc. is a learning process and so the staff, in time, will return the enrichments of such work to the legislature itself and thus Members as a whole will benefit. Administratively these arrangements can be quite difficult but they should always be sought after in the interest of the legislature as a whole. The library should of course act as a service to all staff of the legislature who are about their official duties.

3.05   The question of the relationship between the library and political party staff is more difficult. Central funds for the support of legislatures and the staff of political parties are limited and it can arise that both are competing for limited resources. If therefore these two institutions become too close or their two areas of responsibility too blurred, one or other, and it would often be the library in this case, would receive inadequate support. In turn this would rebound on Members generally and their confidence in the service. There are also many of the same problems that apply to Members' personal staff (see 3.04) when considering the work undertaken by the library and by the staff of political parties which are writ large. There is therefore a definite argument in favour of the library keeping political parties and their staff at arms length and seeing themselves very much as a service for the legislature only and in no way involved in support for Members via political parties. However this again is bound to be influenced by the political culture and traditions of the society.

CHAPTER 4

LIBRARY ORGANISATION AND ADMINISTRATION

4.01   The role of the Librarian in a legislature really depends on two main factors:

1.   The place of the library in the structure of the legislature as a whole, referred to under 3.01 above.

2.   The extent to which there may be developed research services with possibly subject specialists to carry them out and whether any such staff work within the library or are in a different department in the legislative service.

Most legislative library services start out just offering a library and reference service. Many do not go further than this. But some, such as the UK and subsequently Canada and Australia, have added research services to the library and reference services already on offer. The most developed form of such research services for a legislature is to be found in the Congressional Research Service in the US Library of Congress – the work of which forms the basis of Part III of this book – and Japan has a similar arrangement. There would seem to be some dangers in separating administratively the library and reference services from the research services. Firstly there can be confusion for Members as to what their legislative staff mean by terms such as 'reference' and 'research' and this can lead to muddle with regard to enquiries. On the other hand, research staff especially if they are administered separately, may start to duplicate resources and build up small libraries not so much of books as of other materials and this can quickly become expensive and inefficient. In view of the fact that the legislature needs a co-ordinated information service at a number of different levels, there does seem to be a strong argument for one administrative head, whether the post is designated Librarian, Director of Information, Director of Research or some other name. The Librarian may be responsible to the presiding officer or to a legislative official higher up the hierarchy than himself. Whichever it is, it is important for everyone to realise that information services are very expensive to acquire and to sustain and that therefore the Librarian needs to be heard by and therefore have access to a high level of the legislature's administration. If this is not done resources may be inadequate and therefore under used and so ultimately uneconomic.

The Librarian will not only be responsible for administering his staff but will also be playing an important role vis-à-vis other senior colleagues in the legislative service as a whole. But he will need to go further than that. The administration of many legislative services is pretty much centred on the legislature and its Members. Procedural services, reporting of debates services, works, maintenance, security, financing the legislature etc, etc, are by definition centred on the legislature. The information service however while also being centred on Members and their needs is equally, by definition, very conscious of the problems and resources of the outside world. Like Members themselves it is the whole of society and its problems, both national and international, that is the source of its work. The Librarian therefore very much needs to keep a firm base within the legislature but with an open door to the outside world. Once the information service reaches a certain size, in view of this wide responsibility and in view of the long hours the service is often required, the Librarian may need a deputy to share some of the responsibilities.

4.02 Because the legislature's information services are often only for Members, or certainly mostly for Members, it may be appropriate for there to be a Library Committee of Members. They would normally be 'assisted' by the librarian, who may act as the secretary, and apart from being kept informed of developing policy through the Librarian's regular reports, they would be able to advise him of needs from the Members' point of view and warn him if they considered that a proposal or a development was running counter to Members' views. The Librarian would need to work closely with these Members and especially with their Chairman, but Members are very busy people and should certainly not be troubled with the detail of administration, any staff problems etc. etc. The Librarian needs to strike the right balance with his Committee which might meet only a few times a year and he can then find it very helpful in nurturing the Library's relationship with Members.

4.03   Almost every legislature, except possibly Australia in its new Parliament House in Canberra, finds accommodation a problem. The great growth of Members' personal staff has resulted in legislative staff spilling out into old, converted and sometimes new buildings adjacent to the Parliament House itself. The US, Sweden, France, Finland, Norway, Germany and the UK are just a few countries where such growth has been marked. This presents serious difficulties for legislative libraries. It has to be accepted that libraries take up a great deal of space and that although some Members may welcome the relaxation and browsing facility they may offer, as they grow, simply reflecting the importance of information in our societies today, they will have to move further from the legislature. This happened in the US in the 1890s, when the Library of Congress moved out of the Capitol, it has happened in Finland and Norway in recent decades and in the UK at the beginning of the 1990s. Forward planning needs to take such a possibility into account. The Librarian's problem is in this case to ensure two things:

1.   He provides a quick reference and information service on the spot for Members and/or their personal staff and also of course for other legislative staff in relation to their duties. The nearer the chamber of the legislature that this can be offered the more efficient it will be from everybody's point of view.

2.   If he has the remit and thus the staff to offer information services at a deeper level, he must ensure that Members are kept aware of them and that a personal service for them is kept available.

Possibly an ideal solution is to maintain a Members' library available only to them and organised in a welcoming, relaxed way, especially as Members do spend a great deal of time exposed to the public in many different ways, so that the privacy of their library can be of a very real benefit to them. If the library grows to the point when it is split between a Members' library with the other services elsewhere, then the latter should be planned to have the best possible modern communications with the Members' library so that Members are kept sharply aware of the depth of service which is available to them.

4.04 There is nothing particularly distinctive about storage for legislative libraries. If the library has responsibility for the archives then these may need special archival treatment. In some cases the legislative library may have some copyright responsibilities for materials in which case not only must there be space to keep these publications but temperature, humidity etc. must also match archival needs. For the rest it would be expected that modern methods of keeping information would be used and that storage would be secured as close as possible to where Members and the library staff working on their behalf needed it. The Librarian should never pass up an opportunity to put down a marker for storage not only for current needs but also those of his successors.

4.05 The disposal of material is nearly always quite a difficult decision. One important factor is the extent to which the legislative library can secure support from other libraries. These may include government departments, specialist institutes, academic organisations and indeed the public library service. This support is of course not available outside normal working hours and this fact may not always meet the legislature's needs. The disposal of library materials is a very labour intensive job which often discourages people from undertaking it. It is more efficient in staff time to dispose of runs of journals etc rather than individual titles so that union lists of periodicals combined with good relations with neighbourly libraries can help to get quicker results from a disposal programme. All official papers of the legislature will be kept in the appropriate archive.

4.06 The services offered by the legislative library need to be promoted. This is partly because their contribution to improving the quality of the legislature's work needs emphasizing. Unlike other legislative services eg: procedural advice, the reporting of debates, the catering facilities etc which are essential for the organisation to function at all, the information services are chiefly of importance in improving the quality of Members' work. This applies to their relationship with their constituents and their specialised interests as much as it does to their contribution to debate, and their questioning in committee and in the Chamber. Among the more obvious methods of promoting services are noticeboards, racks to display research work, new book lists, photocopies of the little pages of journals, and pamphlets and brochures describing special services. Where modern technology is used for cataloguing and indexing it is now quite easy to 'profile' individual Members interests and to offer them a Selective Dissemination of Information (SDI) service to match their current interests and problems. More generally the range of the service can be set down on video as has been done in the US, Canada, including specifically Ontario, and recently in the UK. There is also, following an election, the well tried methods of offering Members a personal tour and description of the services available. Despite all these obvious methods such is the pressure on Members, especially when they are first elected, it can take a surprisingly long time, sometimes years, before a Member becomes aware of the potential of the information services available to him. It therefore always rests with the staff at every level to excel with the smallest enquiries and thus build up a state of confidence with Members so they may extend their demands and thus reveal the full quality of the service.

REFERENCE SERVICES

Introduction

A legislature's library must have the capacity to respond to the distinctive information needs of Members. In addition to the matter of impartiality discussed earlier (see Part I, 3.03), Members require information which is directly relevant, factually accurate and extremely timely. With regard to the provision of reference services, therefore, selectivity and speed are crucial. These requirements need to be taken into account in planning for and managing the library's human and material resources, which in turn define the character and extent of its services.

Part II of these Guidelines identifies the kinds of materials which ought to be collected and maintained in the legislative library's stock. It also discusses the composition, training and development of requisite staff and addresses fundamental aspects regarding the provision of basic information services to Members.

CHAPTER 5

LIBRARY MATERIALS: THE CORE COLLECTION
AND COLLECTIONS DEVELOPMENT

5.01 In some countries, as for example in Pakistan, the numbers, qualifications and pay scales of staff that any library may employ, are set by law in relation to the size of the collection, which is defined only in terms of the number of books it contains. Such an equation between the size of stock and the size etc. of staff sets a particular problem for legislative libraries which are inclined to be labour intensive because of their active role as information centres. Even in those countries where staffing levels are not dictated by the size or description of the library's collection, there obviously is a relationship not only between the composition of the staff and size of the collection, on the one hand, but also between the content of the collection and the nature of the services to be provided, on the other hand.

The collection, after all, is together with the staff, the very foundation of a library's services. It constitutes the institution's memory and ought, as well, to reflect the needs and interests of the library's users. With specific reference to a legislature's library, it must be understood that unless the collection mirrors the information needs of legislators and is organized in such a manner that relevant materials are readily at hand, even the most competent of staff cannot respond to Members' queries on a timely basis.

5.02 An identification of the various components which form a basic legislative collection, then, must per force be considered at the outset of a discussion of reference services. The five primary categories of items which must be represented are parliamentary documents, official publications, reference books, current affairs materials, and general books on subjects germane to the legislature's statutory responsibilities (see 1.04 and 1.05).

5.03 Parliamentary documents are those materials which the institution itself generates in

17

the course of carrying out its legislative work. These include the rules of procedure and conduct of business; the "calendar" or orders of the day; the record of the proceedings of debates; copies of the bills and motions introduced in the chamber(s); committee reports; copies of questions/interpellations put to the ministries, which are "taken as read" on the floor and consequently do not appear in the printed record of the debates; the journal; and other publications of the legislature. The latter would include such things as informative booklets about the structure, operations and facilities of the legislature, rulings of the chair if separately compiled, a directory of Members, and the like. It is also important to collect certain documents of other parliaments, especially those of the same region of the world or of countries where there is an especially close relationship. These can generally be acquired on an exchange basis. The records of debates, committee reports, and the rules of procedure of other parliaments, for example, can be especially useful.

5.04   It is equally important to have a reasonably comprehensive collection of the official publications of indigenous executive and judicial agencies. This is because in most parliamentary democracies these agencies have a specific responsibility to inform the legislature and its Members. The official gazettes and other statutory compilations are especially critical. In many countries, the library of the national legislature automatically receives such publications under the legal deposit law, but this is not universally so. In those countries where this is not the case, the legislature should be prevailed upon to amend the law accordingly, as these publications contain extremely important information that for the most part is unavailable from any other source. Unfortunately, where they are not received by legal deposit, the library more often than not has to pay the Government's printing office for copies of public documents and frequently does not even receive notice, or at least a regular and complete listing, of the publications of government agencies. On a selective basis, the official publications of foreign governments and international bodies are also significant sources of information which is often vital in the provision of legislative reference services.

5.05   Like all other types of libraries, a legislative library needs a good reference collection.

In view of the fact that Members invariably require accurate and relevant data, sources which are outdated are utterly useless. Thus, it is critically important that the reference collection be maintained on a current basis. It is equally important that this collection be as comprehensive as possible. There are at least twelve categories of materials which are generally incorporated into the reference collection and are also, therefore, not material for loan. These include encyclopedias, dictionaries and thesauri, parliamentary handbooks and procedural manuals as well as other sorts of handbooks and manuals, directories, yearbooks and almanacs, indexes and catalogues, statistical compilations, legal source material, biographical works, quotation sourcebooks, standard bibliographies, atlases, and travel guides.

5.06   In order to represent the concerns of their constituents in the corridors of power and to effect national policy decision–making, Members must stay abreast of current affairs in general and on top of the latest national and world news in particular. Consequently, access to current affairs material is often the primary reason Members come into the legislature's library. Of paramount interest are national and regional newspapers, local magazines and professional journals, news digests, and law reviews. To the extent that budgetary resources permit, it is also important for legislative libraries to subscribe to major or at least representative foreign newspapers and journals, if Members' current information needs are to be well served. Since manual searches of newspapers and periodical publications are extremely time–consuming and even the daily clipping and indexing of such materials is highly labour intensive, subscribing to appropriate commercial indexing services can be a very cost–effective investment. In many countries however, they are not yet widely available.

5.07   In view of the time lag between research and publication, the contents of books generally lack currency. Consequently, books are of relatively lesser importance in a legislative library than the kinds of materials identified above. In fact, they comprise as little as 20–25 per cent of the collections of some of the world's major parliamentary libraries. Nonetheless, they form an integral part of a basic collection. Books on national and world history, law and constitutionalism, and political science certainly should be collected in a fairly comprehensive way. Political biographies and analyses of political institutions are especially important as are books on foreign affairs and international trade. But in most subjects, e.g. economics, the emphasis on book buying is on practice rather than theory. Government and politics is the art of the possible. The collections development policy will, of course, be influenced to a large degree by the particular legislature's power to legislate (see Part I, Chapter 1). However, in most legislatures, whether federal or unitary, Members will need reference to in-depth treatments dealing with national policy formulation on such subjects as agriculture, business and commerce, defence and strategic affairs, economics, education, environment, science and technology, and social welfare, including health services and population planning. In most national legislatures today, debates on more topical but global issues, such as disarmament, drug control and interdiction, international terrorism, nuclear non-proliferation and refugee resettlement, are commonplace. Thus, books on these and similar subjects ought also to be selectively acquired.

Finally, books which cater to the recreational reading pursuits of Members need to be acquired, if sparingly. It not only encourages Members to cultivate the habit of reading but is generally viewed as a welcomed service. In developing countries, where other library resources are sparse, it may in fact constitute a significant service to Members. It helps to bridge any gap between the Member and his information service.

5.08   The collections development policy will necessarily be subject to the considerations of budgetary resources and space constraints. To the extent they can be accommodated however, cartographic materials (i.e. maps, charts, geographical surveys, etc.) are useful additions to the core collection in a legislative library. Materials in audiovisual (AV) format are playing an increasingly important role in legislative collections as well.

The ever-expanding use of AV technology in the worldwide dissemination of information has meant that much useful information is now created and transmitted only in non-print media. Consequently, legislative libraries must also begin, if they are not already doing so, to collect data produced on audio cassettes, film, and videotapes. Indeed, many parliaments are now recording their proceedings of debates on tape recorders if not closed-circuit television systems. In such cases, the primary documentation of the legislature itself is being maintained at least for archival purposes in non-print format, and the library, itself therefore, must gear towards utilising non-print media in the provision of at least some of its information services. (See Chapter 11, 'Mediating News and Public Opinion to Members of Parliament).

5.09   With regard to the organisation and preservation of legislative collections, a word or two is perhaps in order. Various cataloguing and classification schemes are in use in the legislatures of different countries. The appropriate choice as to which scheme to utilise should be predicated upon the norms of use in the other major libraries of the particular country, in order to facilitate interlending and national cooperative cataloguing efforts. However, for the libraries of those national legislatures which are now planning, or looking ahead to the prospect of developing automated information services and which, furthermore, hope to participate in regional and international networks in due course, it is important to take cognizance of the scheme employed in the larger system or network with which the library wants to join and to convert to that scheme earlier rather than later on. This will minimise the problem of the database conversion at the time of linking to the larger information network and thereby substantially reduce both disruption of work and the attendant costs which conversion programmes entail.

5.10   As previously mentioned (see Part I, Chapter 4: 4.04. and 4.05), the matter of determining what is to be retained in a legislative library's collections over what periods of time is affected to some extent by its relationships with other libraries and archives, particularly the national library. The need to provide information to Members during legislative sessions during hours of day when other libraries may be closed is another important factor. In any case, the primary documentation of the legislature itself must be kept as a permanent collection, and a substantial number of official publications of government agencies will likely need to be maintained for an indefinite period. These materials, of course, proliferate exponentially and consume

21

tremendous amounts of space if kept in their printed form. Moreover, given that they are generally printed on an inferior quality of paper and issued without hard covers, it can be quite an expensive proposition to bind and preserve them. For these reasons, the utilisation of micrographics technology is of increasing consequence but not without some controversy.

On the one hand, there are those who argue that Members do not like to sit in front of microform machines to read source material. Moreover, for smaller legislative libraries with extremely limited financial resource and small staffs, mounting full-scale micrographic operations can be prohibitively expensive. On the other hand, there are those who see micrographics as the most viable option for solving the problems previously mentioned. They point to the fact that there are a number of microform reader/printers on the market today which are relatively inexpensive and give reasonably good quality prints. On the other hand there are those who argue that Members seldom need an entire document but only a few pages from such sources, and that it is not often the reference staff who use the microforms to identify and copy relevant portions of data in response to a Member's query. So Members' hesitancy to use microforms need not be a negative consideration. The costs of full-scale micrographic operations is another matter, however, but one which may be approached through a cooperative endeavour with other information organisations, particularly the national library, national archive or, particularly, other legislative libraries in federal systems. In any case, microforms are a cleaner, quicker, and -- over the long term -- much cheaper means of storage and retrieval of documentary materials, and much faster and more cost-effective than clippings files as a means of maintaining newspaper and journal articles for legislative reference purposes.

CHAPTER 6

STAFF: COMPOSITION, QUALIFICATIONS, TRAINING AND DEVELOPMENT

6.01 A number of factors must be considered in defining the numbers and qualifications of staff who may be needed to run a legislature's library. The first determinant is the character of the legislature itself. If it occupies a weak position within the governmental structure and is subservient to a powerful executive body, its Members are highly unlikely to be active users of information with regard to their participation in the business of the house. Whatever use they may make of the library, therefore, is more likely to be of a personal scholarly or recreational nature, requiring very general assistance from the library staff. In such cases, the library is also likely to be quite small and staffed by only one or two people whose duties will be primarily custodial in nature.

If, on the other hand, it is not only a sovereign institution but the pinnacle of the Government's law and decision making apparatus, Members' information needs will undoubtedly be of a more complex nature, requiring the assistance of well educated staff who are themselves sophisticated users of information resources and technologies. Concomitantly, the library will necessarily be of substantial size with respect to both the collections and the level of operations and, hence, be served by a multi-layered staff including professionals, paraprofessionals and clericals.

Most of the world's parliaments and their libraries fall somewhere between these two extremes, the majority of them being relatively small in size but fairly active in character... the more so as the upsurge of democratisation throughout the world including the former Soviet Union, Eastern Europe, South America and parts of Africa, has brought with it a fresh new dynamism in the legislatures. Other determinants, therefore, regarding the composition of the library staff merit thoughtful examination.

6.02 The size of the collection is certainly one of the factors which will determine the composition of the library staff, particularly with respect to the level of technical services as well as the maintenance and preservation of the stock. But, as set out in the previous chapter, staff needs and therefore size should not be measured against merely the number of books in the collection. Rather, the scope and requisite handling of the entire collection must be taken into account, since books constitute a relatively modest proportion of it unless they are the only materials kept on a permanent basis. Although this is sometimes the case, especially where space is severely constrained or funds for the conservation and preservation of other types of materials are lacking, it certainly is not the norm and so should be discounted as the basis for deciding the numbers and qualifications of staff.

6.03   The determinant of far greater importance, which derives from the character of the legislature and dictates the composition of the collections required, is the use Members make of the library. This must be defined in terms of not only the number of questions asked but also the scope and complexity of the queries. If a substantial quantity of the questions coming into the information desk require substantive knowledge and professional acumen to answer, then obviously a sufficient number of appropriately qualified staff will be needed to handle the workload.

6.04   The importance of promoting the services of the library cannot be overemphasised in the context of the preceding paragraph. If Members are not sufficiently aware of the library's capacity to serve their information needs, they are unlikely to avail of the services very often, if at all. At the same time, if the statistics on the Members' use is relatively low, the Librarian's pleas for the requisite posts to provide appropriate services will probably fall on deaf ears. This necessarily will preclude the library from being able to offer the services of which Members would avail if only there were competent staff to provide them.

6.05   There also tends to be a direct relationship between the qualifications of the information services staff and the kind of use Members make of the library. Where the staff are professionally competent, they are able to help Members frame their queries in a manner which ensures the likelihood that they will receive more highly relevant information. This, in turn, inspires the confidence of the Members in the library's information services and invariably leads to a higher rate of use. It can be seen then, that, especially if the staff is small, it must be competent and motivated to give service.

6.06   There are no magic numbers with regard to how many staff are needed, since it relates more to the quality and extent of the services rather than the size and diversity of the collections. It must be pointed out, however, that more professional staff will be required in those legislatures where the library has the responsibility of supporting the legislative work of committees as well as the information needs of individual Members. This, of course, is also affected by the scope of the committees' work and whether or not they have their own staff support. A further discussion of this topic is presented in Part III.

6.07   While there obviously are similarities between reference work as it is carried on in any library and as it is practised in legislative libraries, specialised training generally is required for fresh entrants into parliamentary information services. Remembering that speed, currency, relevance, and accuracy are the hallmarks of Member needs, the reference services staff must become thoroughly familiar with the organisation and the scope of the entire collections and with the relevant finding aids so that valuable time is not lost when a Member needs assistance. They also should have expert knowledge of the structure, operations, rules and procedures of the legislature and all of its various branches. Additionally, they must have a particular sensitivity to the impartiality and the confidentiality with which they are expected to handle Member's information requests.

6.08   The sort of training needed to meet the requirements described above is generally imparted on the job by the Librarian, in the case of the smaller libraries, or by one of the more experienced staff in the medium sized to larger libraries. More formal methods of staff development may include continuing education and upward mobility programmes as well as participation in seminars, workshops, and skills training institutes. It is also important to allow professional staff the opportunity from time to time to attend library association conferences and selectively to visit other legislative and research libraries.

6.09 There are "pros and cons" regarding the efficacy of sending staff to other national legislatures for in service training. There are undoubtedly benefits to both institutions which come through such cross–cultural experiences in terms of enhancing mutual understanding of the resources and operations of the respective parliaments and promoting cooperation between their libraries. Provided that the trainee has reasonable facility in the language of the host institution, sufficient background and skill to participate in its work, and the ability to adapt to living in a foreign culture, the trainee can derive useful insights from exposure to the methodologies and procedures utilised by their colleagues in other legislatures.

All that having been said, however, very few such experiences have been genuinely profitable for either the individual trainee or the trainee's own institution. In most cases, the transfer of knowledge is at best minimal. There are a number of reasons why this is so. First, foreign language comprehension is a very real barrier for the majority of trainees. Changes in time, climate, food, and one's physical and social environment – generally referred to as culture shock – also inhibit to one degree or another the trainee's ability fully to concentrate on the learning experience. Unfortunately, the time and effort which a host institution must invest in order for such training to be of any significant value is a substantial drain on its ability to fulfil its own mission. Therefore, the training period is frequently limited to such a short duration that the trainee simply does not have enough time to make the necessary adjustments to the strangeness of a different working environment. Perhaps the greatest impediment, however, is the fact that in most cases the trainee is from a smaller, less well-equipped and understaffed library, whereas the host organisation is most likely to be a larger, well–developed legislative information service with highly specialised staff utilising the latest technologies in the provision of even the most basic information services. Naturally, a trainee from a country in which electricity and telephones may be considered luxuries can take home very little applied knowledge from his or her brief experience with automated information storage and retrieval systems.

6.10 It would be far more helpful for a developing library to have an experienced cataloguer, acquisitions specialist, reference librarian or preservation technician come to work in its library for one to three months in order to give practical day to day guidance and assistance in the local environment. It would also be more affordable. The cost of air transportation would be the same in either case, but the local costs would be considerably less for the foreign trainer staying in a developing country than for the foreign trainee visiting a developed country. More consideration ought to be given to this option, including the possibility of having colleagues from legislatures of neighbouring countries in the region participate, since most of them would be at similar levels of operations, services, and environmental conditions as those at the training site.

CHAPTER 7

PRIMARY SERVICES

7.01   Even if a piece of work is substantively accurate and responsive to a Member's request, it is completely irrelevant if it is not delivered to the Member in time to be of use. It is imperative, therefore, that all of the library's human, material and physical resources be focused to meet this requirement. The staff must be honed not merely to respond when asked but to anticipate the kinds of questions that are likely to come as a debate progresses or a public crisis erupts. Furthermore, they should be prepared to distribute pertinent handouts to interested Members on fast–breaking issues and as a matter of routine to pass on to Members who regularly use the library information concerning subjects known to be of interest to them. In short, the staff should be active purveyors of information rather than passive custodians of materials which are of no practical value if not put to use in supporting the day–to–day work of the legislature.

7.02   The focal point of reference services is generally the information desk, although, if the library provides it, a telephone "hot–line" may be nearly as important in the provision of on–demand services. Except in the very few legislatures which have totally integrated on–line systems, including such facilities as electronic mail, it is crucial that the information desk be centrally located as near to the chamber as possible, in order to accommodate the frenetic schedules which most Members must keep during legislative sessions.

7.03   The information desk serves at least two very important functions. The first is the thoughtful "negotiation" of inquiries requiring extensive treatment so as to ensure that all the pertinent details related to the Member's request are recorded, particularly if they are passed on to some other staff member or unit for response. The second is to provide assistance to Members in their use of the library and to give help on–the–spot with specific queries which require quick factual answers.

In order to accomplish the second task, the information desk must have essential finding aids and primary reference sources at hand or immediately adjacent to it. If the library has two or more professional staff, they should rotate duty at the information desk. The time spent at the information desk shows them the most urgent matters claiming the attention of Members, while the hours spent away from it allows them to review the new materials coming into the library and, thus, enables them to stay abreast of current sources of relevant data.

7.04 Another important centre of activity in the library is the circulation, or lending desk. In the very smallest libraries, the circulation function may in fact be handled at the information desk; but it is desirable to carry out these two activities at separate points where it is feasible to do so. The charging and discharging of books is an important but fairly routine task that can be handled with reasonable ease by clerical staff. Maintaining accurate charge records is very important, however, in order that the whereabouts of an item in circulation can be readily ascertained when there is urgent demand for it.

7.05 Many other reference service activities take place at some distance from these two reader assistance points. One of the most common of these is locating and photocopying items from the press clippings and pamphlet files. Of course, this presupposes that the library has sufficient staff to assign someone the task of clipping and indexing articles from the daily newspapers on a routine basis. Preparing listings of new additions to the library's collections, producing topical bibliographies on important issues, and compiling relevant background materials which may be incorporated into information packets for general distribution to Members are other significant activities. The reference staff also frequently have to undertake extensive or very precise literature searches, sometimes consulting colleagues in other libraries for help in identifying pertinent sources. They may also reciprocate by providing assistance to other libraries needing information about the legislature or from sources which may be uniquely held by the legislative library.

7.06 Closely related but somewhat distinct from the above is the provision of current awareness or "selective dissemination of information" (SDI) services. As suggested earlier in the context of promoting the library's services (see Part I, 4.06), this activity is routinely and efficiently carried on in those legislative libraries having an automated system. Even without computers and micrographic equipment, however, such services can be provided, even if on a modest scale. the distinctive characteristics of this type of service is that it is periodic (usually but not necessarily fortnightly) and that it caters to the Members' requirement to stay informed about subjects of continuing interest, particularly as they may relate to their committee assignments or to governmental policy–making in matters of long–term concern to their respective constituencies.

Essentially what this service entails is routinely providing references to the latest periodical articles, reports, and documents which correspond to the specific topics of each Member's interest. Where a library's staff and resources permit, it can and is actually meant to be highly selective and, therefore, of significant benefit to Members, whose reading time is generally limited by the pressures of other work.

7.07   In a generic sense, an SDI service is a specialised version of a current awareness service, which does not necessarily have such a selective focus. It can simply be the provision of photocopies of the title pages of journals, pamphlets, reports and documents, although the distribution of the photocopies can be done somewhat selectively. It can also include photocopies of important news features taken from the files of recent press clippings. There are however two aspects of SDI work which need careful consideration. First it is important that the 'profile' of a Member's interests is kept up–to–date by being regularly revised because the pressures on a Member and therefore his/her interests and needs change. Secondly, SDI can lead to excessive demand for photocopying and publications. In both cases the service can become wasteful.

7.08   In addition to the range of information services described above, there are a number of special services which are provided in varying degrees by some legislative libraries, although by no means all of them. Perhaps the most important of these is Member education, which can be variously defined as comprising a basic orientation programme to familiarise new Members with the organisation, rules of procedures and services of the legislature or as consisting if a fairly comprehensive programme of seminars and workshops on a host of substantive issues, aimed at all interested Members and conducted throughout the legislative year.

The library (or legislative information service) may be the focal point of such programmes, particularly in those legislatures where research services are integrated with library services in a single entity of the legislature's organisational structure, or it may be a participant along with other support branches of the legislature. In either case, the purpose of Member education programmes is to provide them with requisite knowledge and skills to execute properly their duties as legislators and to enable them to make effective use of the institutional facilities and resources of the legislature.

7.09 Responding to queries from the public is another special category of reference services and is a particularly sensitive one, especially in those legislatures having limited staff and resources. Where provision for services to the public exists at all, it is fairly restrictive. Nonetheless, legislative libraries are generally obliged to provide public information services in some manner, if comprising nothing more than informative brochures about the legislature and its activities. In some cases, limited access is provided directly to the public, while in others information is disseminated indirectly in support of Members' constituent services (See the discussion in Part I, 2.03 and 2.04).

7.10 Video services are taking on increasing importance as a special information service of legislative libraries. These may consist merely of providing monitors in some convenient location within the precincts of the library for viewing/listening to AV materials collected by the library, or they may amount to full-sale production of audio visual programmes to support Member education and/or public orientation programmes. While video services are generally only to be found in the more well-developed parliaments, they could play a very significant role in even the smallest legislatures of developing countries, as it is not uncommon for some of their Members to be illiterate or neo–literate and, therefore, unable to utilise the traditional services of the library. At a minimum what is needed is a television set and video cassette player and access to AV materials which are likely to be available in other nearby libraries or information centres. This matter is considered in Chapter 11 of Mediating News and Public Opinion to Members of Parliament.

7.11   Mounting exhibits is yet another specialised information activity of many legislative libraries. This ranges from small displays of items from the collections, attractively arranged in the library's foyer or reading room to mark an important event in the history of the legislature or the nation, to the maintenance of a parliamentary museum, as for example in the National Assembly of Thailand, in Tokyo and in Warsaw. Museum operations obviously require ample funds and specially qualified staff, but they can be quite important in projecting the role of the legislature in the nation's life, especially to visiting classes of schoolchildren. In the United Kingdom House of Commons this role is carried still further through the work of an Education Unit covering the work of Parliament and which is part of the Library Department.

PART III

RESEARCH SERVICES

Introduction

Research services, per se, do not exist in many legislatures or, where they do, are not necessarily linked directly with the library in a single organisational entity. They are sometimes administered as a separate branch of the legislature and may even be associated strictly with parliamentary groups rather than being part of the non-partisan institutional services. Where research services are linked with these party groups, then an impartial research service for legislators is clearly impossible. Again, the character of the legislature itself and the form of government (i.e. federal or unitary) influence both the definition and the organisation of the legislative research services. However, it can be observed that they tend to be more dynamic and generally more extensive and more economic in those legislatures where they are directly linked with the library service.

Part III of the Guidelines examines the collections of materials in terms of the requirements in support of research, (Chapter 8) the composition of the staff needed to perform analytical work, (Chapter 9) and the nature and range of research services utilised in a legislature (Chapter 10).

CHAPTER 8

RESEARCH: COLLECTIONS

8.01 **Introduction**

The library collection does not have to be especially large in order adequately to support legislative research services. Rather, the collections development effort needs to be focused on areas of relevant subject specialisation. Still, the collection has to be sizeable enough to ensure that it is reasonably comprehensive in the subject areas of primary concern to the respective legislature.

8.02 In pursuing these objectives it is vitally important to have appropriate acquisition source materials coming into the library on a regular basis. An outdated copy of *Books in Print* and a few scattered issues of publishers' catalogues will not sustain the necessary acquisitions effort. Nor will it do to wait passively for the receipt of the next issue of the local book distributors' list and merely check off all of the items being offered that happen to contain in their titles words which seem to match the bucket terms list. At the very least, such items should be requested on approval, so that their contents can be examined and, if found irrelevant, the items can be returned. This is the best method of acquisition because in the first place, titles can be and indeed frequently are misleading. Secondly, imprudently spending the acquisitions budget simply on whatever is being offered at the time may preclude the purchase later on of a more expensive but more relevant treatment of an extremely important issue. In short, the matter of careful selection of materials when building up a research collection cannot be overemphasised.

8.03 The research staff themselves, when they are part of the Parliamentary service, are a key resource in the collections development effort and they ought to play an active role in it. In the normal course of their professional reading, they see references to significant books and studies in their respective fields. Most professional journals contain a book review section, and all scholarly books and articles include some sort of bibliographical references (i.e. footnotes, chapter notes, or bibliographies). Providing the library staff with citations to such references is an invaluable aid. The research staff should also be consulted in determining the selection criteria and should be asked to examine materials obtained on approval.

8.04 Very few, if any, of even the largest legislative libraries can afford to acquire everything their research staffs might need in the course of their work. Even if they have ample acquisitions funds, they are generally faced with severe space constraints. So, whether large or small, the library must have a rational collections development policy. An important consideration in this regard is interlibrary cooperation, especially with the national library and other research or special libraries.

Because legislative libraries generally find it necessary to restrict public access to their facilities and collections, they tend not to participate in union cataloguing programmes and, in some cases, even interlibrary lending arrangements. However, for smaller libraries, especially those in developing countries where library materials of all sorts are in short supply, cooperation in such endeavour should be considered in a positive vein. Indeed until such libraries are well established, it can be regarded as essential. In most cases libraries and information services are most cooperative with the library of the legislature. As in the example of Finland (See Part 1, Chapter 2: 2.02), formal or informal agreements between the legislative library and one or two other major libraries regarding a division of labour in building and servicing preeminent collections in specific subject areas can well benefit a nation, along with the legislature and its research programme.

8.05 Whatever the size and comprehensiveness of the collection may be, its usefulness for research purposes is limited unless it has been indexed to a high degree of specificity. This may mean assigning six or more subject terms to the bibliographic record in some instances. The decision as to what subject authority list to use is a crucial one, particularly if there is no staff member with expert indexing skills. Without a relevant compendium of subject terms, it is quite unlikely that the collections can be indexed at the level of detail required to support a legislative research programme. Some of the more highly developed legislative libraries have created specialised thesauri as a complement to their development of automated information systems (See Part IV Chapter 12 and 13). Any of these would serve the general purpose of a smaller sister library, if translated into the relevant national language and suitably adapted as necessary to the local socio–political culture.

8.06 Depending on the physical location of the research service as well as its organisational location, consideration may have to be given to maintaining separate collections within each research unit (or office in the case of the smaller services). The size of such collections will also depend on the number of staff and the workload of the respective units as well as, of course, the source and availability of funds. If the research service is a separate branch of the legislative service, then presumably it will have its own budget head for the purpose or else the library's budget will be given an additional allocation to cater for this research requirement. In either case, if funds are limited and duplicate copies of books needed for the library's general collections as well as the research units, materials frequently needed by the research staff and those which are highly specialised sources would most logically be assigned on "permanent loan," as it were, to the respective research staff members. Otherwise, they will be greatly hindered in performing their work in a timely manner, and this would constitute a disservice to the Members.

8.07 **Management of the Collections**

Overseeing the management of the research collection may be the responsibility of a professional librarian, one of the researchers or a clerk. At Westminster, for instance, each of the seven research sections has a sub–library run by professional librarians with qualifications distinct from those of the researchers in the sections. This person may report directly to the head of the research section as a whole or, if it is a very large research service that has numerous divisions, they may report to the head of the specific division served by their collection. If the research section is affiliated with a parliamentary library or some other library, there may be a more complicated reporting structure in place that directly involves the library or some mechanism for working closely with the library regarding policies, acquisitions, etc.

8.08   The usefulness of a legislative research collection depends less on its size than on the careful selection and focus of the materials. It is true that the size of a legislative research collection will to some extent reflect that of the research and analysis section it serves – a large research section with many areas of subject specialization and a large output necessarily demanding a somewhat larger collection than a smaller unit with a less diverse capacity and a small production. But it should not be assumed that, in order adequately to support a research service, a legislative research collection need emulate the large collection, for example, of a university research library. Unlike such a research library which is often obliged to purchase as much as possible in any given area of specialization, a legislative research collection can afford to be, indeed should be, much more selective. The most used materials in a legislative research collection will often be the most current and, therefore, with some exceptions, the collection does not need to maintain or acquire a large historic collection. Other than concerning the legislature itself, its Members and subjects such as elections and to a degree politics, neither the remit nor the perspective of the work of the legislature's information service is historical. Additionally, the information required to support the up–to–the–minute research needed for a legislative body is often obtained not through publications but by direct contact with others in the field in research institutions, academia, or government agencies.

8.09   **Collections and Collection Policy**

A collection for a research and analysis unit may contain serials, monographs, parliamentary publications, government documents, inter–governmental organisation publications, foreign official publications, association publications, and "grey" literature. ("Grey" literature is extant, sometimes unpublished information which is not covered in any standard sources that review or advertise published works.) The format may range from paper to microfilm to on–line CD–ROM. The information contained in these publications typically covers legislative/legal information; texts of

37

local, national, international newspapers; legislative hearings and daily records; corporate and financial records; international trade statistics; commercial, government, and legislative documents. Regardless of the size of the research collection, it is probably safe to say that its core everyday collection will consist of legal and legislative documents pertaining to the country or state it serves.

Besides legal and legislative documents, statistical sources are playing an increasingly important role in a parliamentary library's collection. Members frequently draw on statistics, not only in the course of drafting legislation, but also to make their point in speeches, debates, etc. The type of statistical information requested can range from the most current figures available to a comparative analysis spread over a long period of time. Most countries publish compendia of statistical information covering a wide range of subjects, e.g., *Statistical Abstract of the United States* and these sources are often invaluable in answering historical questions. However, because of the lag–time in publication, it is usually necessary to call executive departments, associations, or other sources to obtain the most–up–to–date figures. To help offset this time lag, executive agencies in some countries now produce and distribute computerized databases (e.g., *The Economic Bulletin Board* produced by the Office of Business Analysis, U.S. Department of Commerce which contains almost 2,000 different files from the major economic agencies of the U.S. federal government) or CD–ROM discs that are updated frequently (e.g., *The National Trade Data Bank (NTDB)* of the U.S. Department of Commerce). Any successful research or analysis section will need a comprehensive, current core collection of basic materials in the subject areas of primary concern to the respective legislature. A well–developed and carefully thought–out collections development policy is therefore of primary importance. Without a clearly stated policy framework, it is very difficult to identify key requirements, focus acquisitions activity, and obtain currently relevant materials.

A collections development policy can be a very simple or a very complicated document, depending on the size of the research collections budget and the scope of research activity. It can range from a one–page statement to a multi–page document. But formulating a clear, established policy is as important for a small legislative research and analysis section as it is for a large one. A good collections development policy helps hold down costs by assessing the needs of the clientele served, prioritizing their needs, and laying out clear guidelines for the materials to be acquired. While a collections development policy will naturally be focused around the basic and recurring areas of research performed by the research and analysis unit, it should also be reassessed each legislative session in order to reflect the more specific and immediate issues that will concern the legislative body that session.

In choosing materials for a research collection, parliamentary libraries should consider turning for help and guidance to those larger parliamentary libraries that are linked to well-established research divisions, such as the Congressional Research Service or the Deutscher Bundestag. The Congressional Research Service has prepared a *Parliamentary Reference Library Bibliography of Core Materials*. This bibliography was compiled to assist the newly-established parliamentary libraries in Eastern Europe, but the citations in the publication are of interest to any library establishing a reference/research collection.

It should be re-emphasised that the research staff is a key resource in collections development. Ideally, any collections development policy for a research collection should be a collaborative effort involving both librarians (if possible) and researchers, each side bringing its own expertise to bear on the problems encountered.

In formulating a collections development policy it is necessary to distinguish between those publications that will be so heavily and frequently used that they need to be purchased as permanent items in the collection and those items that may be of interest, but are not essential and can be accessed via other libraries' collections. No library can afford to purchase everything it wants (even if it had the space to store it). All libraries are being forced to supplement their own collections in creative ways.

Any acquisitions policy for a research and analysis unit of a legislative body must strive to be pro-active rather than re-active, must cast as wide a net as possible, and must be creative in exploring different ways to acquire publications. Both standard

39

and creative new sources should be explored in the acquisitions process. The traditional procedure of scanning publishers' catalogues, lists of titles in print, library journals, and book reviews in newspapers, library journals, journals and international magazines should, of course, be pursued. For those libraries that can afford it, there are also subscriptions to vendor Selective Dissemination of Information (SDI) services; with these the library can elect to receive bibliographic citations, the publication on approval, or even (more recently), an abstract of the publication in question.

Not only should the standard sources outlined above be utilized but other resources and expertise should be employed to the fullest extent. Here it is especially important to include in the acquisitions process the research specialist or librarian. They will be current concerning scholarly publications reviewed only in professional journals. More important in many cases, the researcher or subject librarian is also able to identify and recommend unpublished studies or "grey" literature.

"Grey" literature occurs in many areas and is of special interest to legislative research units as it is frequently produced by large associations, think–tanks, or special interest groups for in–house consumption. It is, therefore, often an excellent source of up–to–date information and statistics. Because it is not referred to in any standard sources that review or advertise published works, it often poses a special problem for the acquisitions process. However, the researchers and librarians may maintain close contact with think–tanks, special interest groups, and associations in the course of their day–to–day activities, and hence are aware of and can recommend this "grey" literature. If specific organizations and associations produce in–house documents that are consistently useful for the research collection, it even may be possible to work out an informal exchange of materials between the research collection or affiliated legislative library and the organization concerned.

8.10   Library Co–operation

As mentioned in the Introduction to this Chapter 8.04 the size of a legislative research collection can be greatly augmented by interlibrary loan (ILL). ILL is often an economic way to handle the researcher's need to substantiate a point (a quotation, statistic, etc.) without investing in a permanent addition to the collection.   For any sharing arrangement such as ILL to be successful, of course, there must be benefits to all, and no one library or collection should be overburdened. Moreover, it should be remembered that given the short deadlines often placed on legislative research sections, great care should be taken in deciding what materials may be loaned and what must stay in the permanent collection. In this context the growing availability of FAX is increasingly important.

8.11   Newspaper Cuttings

The work of legislative researchers frequently requires a news clippings service, which augments the research collection. A clippings service can provide the researcher with subject organized access to articles from a wide range of newspapers and also periodicals. If the clippings service is routed on a daily basis to the researchers, it can be seen as a collective dissemination of information (SDI) tool. A clippings service can be very costly in terms of both labour and space. In some countries it is now possible to avoid providing this service in-house as there are commercial on-line clippings databases, such as PROFILE.

Careful consideration must also be given to the subject headings under which the clippings will be grouped. The decision as to what subject authority list to use is crucial, particularly if there is no staff member with expert indexing skills. Some of the larger legislative libraries with computerized information systems have created specialised thesauri. These thesauri might serve as a guide to smaller legislative libraries. But these thesauri can only be used as a guide. They cannot be taken whole, but must be adapted and amended to fit each clippings service's unique collection and coverage. A small collection will need to assess their own collection and make up subject headings accordingly. Access to the clippings file for the researcher can vary from a simple paper printed index of major topic headings to on-line complete citations accessed via many different subject headings. This on-line citation may even include an abstract. It is extremely important that any new terms used in thesauri/indexing whether for materials generally or as mentioned here for cuttings should be brought to the attention of the researchers, as these new terms are often linked to an upsurge in legislative interest in a given subject area. The media, including newspapers, often invent new terms under which current issues will be known and these terms therefore need indexing.

8.12 Collections Organisation

Given the tight deadlines under which many legislative research bureaux operate and the constant demand for an immediate response, it is vital that the materials in any research collection be quickly accessible to the researcher. However, from a budgetary standpoint it is also important to avoid duplication of materials where possible, and so a balance has to be struck between these two, sometimes opposing, needs.

How the research collections are located and organized will vary from research section to research section depending on the size of the service. A smaller legislative research unit occupying a relatively limited, cohesive space might choose to have only one central, research collection that will be accessible to all the researchers, thus avoiding duplication of sources. In some very large establishments with numerous research divisions, the different divisions may even choose to organize their collections along different lines. The organization may range from a more formal, central collection to one where each subject researcher keeps their own subject collection at or near their desk, with a small core of reference sources kept in a central location. While the latter probably provides the ultimate in terms of accessibility to the researcher, the drawback is that it can be more expensive and result in duplication of publications. Moreover, individualized collections are less readily accessible to other researchers, who will have difficulty knowing what is available and where it is located. This can cause difficulty when specific specialist information is needed at short notice and a researcher is away.

In order to make sure that these separate research collections are known to the research staff as a whole in case they should need to consult them, many research bureaux publish accession lists for serials and monographs, or have computerized databases to catalogue, index and keep track of their publications. It is important that researchers are constantly informed of new products that have been acquired or produced in-house. An ideal situation would be if newly-acquired materials for the research sections are published in some source or incorporated in any publications put out by the legislative libraries listing their new services, policies and new collections.

Those research and analysis units that are closely connected to legislative or other libraries can benefit from any ILL, depository or copyright status the legislative library or national library enjoys and may not need to enter into their own agreements with other libraries or research institutions.

Legislative research sections that are located in countries that are federations should explore the possibilities of library cooperation between the parliamentary library and the state legislative assembly libraries. They are presently exploring potential agreements of this nature in Malaysia. This is likely to be particularly fruitful as the state libraries have access to state laws that are often important in legislative research at the national level and vice versa. Such cooperation may also save effort through avoiding duplication.

8.13   International Co-operation

Parliamentary libraries have been especially active in working out other ways to help supplement their collections and, at the same time, those of the research service, either based on formal agreements or more informal practices. Sometimes these groupings of libraries have been worked out over the years, based on geographic proximity and closeness of language, such as that of the Nordic parliamentary libraries (Oslo, Copenhagen, Reykjavik, Stockholm, and Helsinki) which work closely together to exchange newly-published records and documents of the parliaments, government communications, and statistical publications. Regional cooperative exchange efforts have also been fostered by regional library associations, such as the Association of

Parliamentary Librarians of Asia and the Pacific (APLAP) and the European Centre for Parliamentary Research and Documentation (ECPRD). Such cooperation can often speed up the securing of information from foreign countries which legislators often need.

Many legislative libraries belong to Inter–Library Lending (ILL) groups. For example, the Folketingets Bibliotek, Arkiv in Denmark is part of a nation–wide library system or a consortium and the Swedish parliamentary library belongs to a consortium consisting of university and specialist libraries.

Those research services not affiliated with a parliamentary or other library may want to consider the potential advantages of arranging ILL agreements with other libraries or research institutions, or even participating in a network of libraries or research collections. Networks are generally based on specific, written contracts covering not only what is to be shared, but also what will be acquired jointly, issues of bibliographic control, and conditions of use.

In the same way that a research section can benefit by being affiliated to a library that has ILL agreements, it can also benefit if that library has depository status or receives materials through the deposit provisions of copyright acts. In both instances this means that the researchers will usually have quick and easy access to a very wide variety of published materials. Sometimes it is possible to transfer the materials from the library to the research collection. But, even where this is not possible, the research section benefits by having a broad idea of what is being published and having the opportunity to examine publications "hands on" to see if they should be purchased as a permanent addition to the research collection.

CHAPTER 9

RESEARCH: STAFFING AND ORGANISATION

9.01 **Introduction**

The number of staff and their required skills are determined primarily by the functions of the legislature they serve and the organisational charter for the research service. Staffing and skill requirements also depend on the relationship of research services to reference services, and to the existence of other support units for the legislature.

9.02 As far as possible the research services should be directly linked with the reference services, whether they both fall under the administrative control of The Librarian or whether the head(s) of library services (i.e. reference and technical processing) and the head(s) of research services (i.e. different subject units) come under a director of a unified branch, variously called the Library and Research Service, the Research and Legislative Information Service, the Documentation and Reference Services Centre, the Congressional Research Service, or under two different departments of the legislature's service. This linking is on the grounds of efficiency and economy and is designed to avoid as far as is practical the duplication of information services for Members.

9.03 In the larger legislatures, committees, in particular committees of enquiry, generally tend to have their own professional as well as clerical support staff, although staff from the research service may be deputed to committees on a temporary basis from time to time and may otherwise assist with major legislative studies. The secretariats of most legislatures, however, lack the means of providing anything more in the way of staff support to committees than stenographic and administrative assistance. As a rule, therefore, a substantial portion of the work undertaken by the research staff may well be in support of the legislative business of both standing and special committees.

9.04 Because of the substantive nature of the work and the requirement for dispassionate

45

assessments of various policy options, people with strong academic credentials as subject specialists and, certainly at senior levels, with relevant research experience and noteworthy publication credits as well, are needed to fill the professional posts in a legislature's research service. These posts are usually at higher pay scales than other staff or carry special stipends in order to recruit and retain suitably qualified personnel. The difference in pay and prospects between library staff and research staff needs to be watched carefully in the context of the overall management of these services. In the House of Commons Library at Westminster, for instance, staff throughout the Library Department including research staff are all part of a unified grading structure, although there are more higher-grade staff in the research service than in the library service.

9.05 Depending on the relationship between the reference and the research staff and on the quantity and level of work to be performed, the professional research staff may be supported by junior research staff who serve as research assistants. In some cases, university students may also be associated with the research group for limited periods as interns. The research group will generally have its own clerical support staff and may employ its own editorial assistants as well. The composition and numerical strength of research staff will depend on the range of subject specialisation required and on the type and volume of Members' and committees' requests for research assistance.

9.06 As in the case of the reference staff, individuals freshly recruited to the research service will need to acquire an intimate familiarity with the legislature's organisation and rules of procedure. They will also need a detailed orientation to the library's collections and finding aids. In fact, some legislative research services require their new staff to rotate through the reference service units during their first few weeks on the job, so that they become thoroughly knowledgeable of the library's resources and activities and well-acquainted with the reference staff. Since they are meant to be specialists, they should presumably already possess relevant job skills in research methodology. However, as it is important for them to stay abreast of their subject specialisations, they ought especially to be encouraged actively to participate in their respective professional associations and to attend and present papers at national and international seminars and conferences in their subject fields.

9.07 Staff exchanges with other legislative research services can be a useful means of staff and organisational development, particularly in the case of nascent parliamentary services. However, they need to be of one to three months duration to be of any significant or lasting value. Such exchanges have also been found to be mutually beneficial in facilitating joint research and publication projects on issues of major bilateral concern.

9.08 Consideration ought to be given to the fact that research staff need to be able to take extended study leave at reasonable periodic intervals in order to update and expand their substantive knowledge and to refresh themselves as scholars. It is important not only for the individuals but also for the respective legislature that its research specialists stay at the top of their form and maintain creditable reputations among their colleagues in the broader professional community. Sabbaticals after every five to seven years provide them with the opportunity to undertake primary research, which both the nature and the pressure of work in the legislative arena preclude. Staff tend to return from such experiences with fresh insights and perspectives which can be usefully brought to bear on public policy decision-making and, thus, gives them renewed enthusiasm for their work in support of the legislature's business.

9.09 **Congressional Research Service**

It might be useful to explore a concrete example of a research service for a legislature in order to trace the combined effects of the role aspirations of the legislature in the governmental system, research unit charter, and the availability of other research providers on the staffing requirements for legislative research. The U.S. Congress requires a large research staff with a wide array of specialized skills because it strives to operate more independently of the executive than is true of most parliamentary systems. It has also given its principal legislative research organization, the Congressional Research Service (CRS), the responsibility of developing alternative

47

policies to those offered by the President and of tracing the consequences and effects of any alternative policy proposals. The CRS charter of services includes information as well as research (the scope of services is discussed more fully in chapter 10) to support Congress in both its policymaking and representational roles. For all its requirements, CRS is comparatively leaner in scientific staffing because of the existence of another legislative support agency – the Office of Technology Assessment. Despite its large research commitment, CRS also has a number of professional librarians (nearly 200) because it has chosen to incorporate reference functions along with its research responsibilities in the same organization.

9.10 Legislative Models

There is a continuum of theoretical models for legislative functioning to use as a guide in selecting the appropriate role and staffing for the legislative research organization. At one end of the continuum is the *functioning legislature*. This body has a small staff and little automation equipment, but sufficient organizational and procedural development to process legislative demands on a reasonably expeditious basis, and enough information to validate policies made elsewhere in government. If a legislative research staff exists, its function is to be a source of information for direct use by legislators with very little in the way of additional personalized professional services – providing self–help reading rooms, basic sources of information for direct perusal by the members, perhaps preparing a few bibliographies and other guides to sources, and transmitting information from executive authorities and other sources. A small number of research staff may be present in one or two high–priority areas.

Then there is the *informed legislature* which has moved beyond the functioning legislature by adding personal staff for the individual legislator to enhance his or her effectiveness, procured computers and other telecommunications equipment that can significantly improve information processing for the legislature, and, if procedures permit, developed the legislative committee process as a means of deepening the substantive and political analysis done in the legislature. Central research staff provide annotated bibliographies, create summaries of bills, provide ready–reference responses to inquiries of the legislators, describe policies and proposals of the government, and offer pro–con assessments. Some of the more advanced research units in this category may trace impacts of proposed policies and generate alternative choices for the legislature.

Finally, at the high end of the continuum in terms of information and staffing requirements, is the *independent legislature*. At this level, specialized expertise has been added to legislative offices, party factions, committee cadres, and central analytic staff; data bases and computer models are developed and used in the legislature; and research services staff are capable of producing long–range projections, developing computer simulation models, carrying out interdisciplinary analyses, and fashioning fully developed options that make independent action by the legislature possible without assistance from the executive or ministries.

9.11   Choosing an Appropriate Model

Each society must choose how far it wishes to pursue independence of legislative action based on its own history and political culture. The choice of design for a legislative research facility might be affected by a number of considerations, beginning with the question of what is the desired degree of independent action by the legislature. Following this decision, a number of related choices regarding institutional capacity will then follow:

How independent? The choices outlined in the models discussed in 9.10 above will condition how large the research enterprise should be, the kinds of staff skills that will need to be acquired, and the kinds of products to be produced. Ultimately, the types of products and services the legislature will need depend on its role aspirations.

Whom to serve? The number of research staff will also depend on who and how many are authorized to use the research services. At a minimum, serving the legislature means offering services on an equitable basis for both opposition members as well as those of the governing party or coalition. In fact, in some parliamentary systems there is a pattern of heavier use of legislative research services by backbenchers and the opposition parties – with those closer to the cabinet or government relying more heavily on the ministries or executive for their information. There is a case to be made for more aggressive service offerings to all elements of the parliament, including the ruling party, based on the premise that the legislature has a unique contribution to make to the public policymaking process – whether that system is presidential or parliamentary in design. It is the role of the executive branch or "government" to develop policies that are in the broad general interest. It is the role of the legislature to screen that public interest and test it against the particular interests of the local groups or areas represented as constituencies by the legislators in the parliament.

In the ensuing dialogue, accommodations will be made that (ideally) preserve the national interest, but arrive at some equitable adjustments to potentially injured or disadvantaged parties. Thus, even committees of the legislature and members of the majority party will benefit from independent analysis and information that permits the legislature to engage in a constructive dialogue on the policies proposed by the ministries.

As already mentioned if research services are provided to legislative committees, then a higher level of staff expertise will be needed to meet their more specialized requirements. This is particularly true where the committees already have considerable expert staff available to them as is the case with the German Bundestag and the U.S. Congress. Generally, the higher the level of expertise of the committee requestor, the greater are the skills needed by the research staff to meet their high expectations and requirements. However, even under systems where professional staffing for committees is relatively spartan, the demands placed on parliamentary research services may be substantial, including on occasion the request to loan research staff to the committee to carry out its functions – covering a broad range of research and general services. Care should be taken to protect limited staff resources from being completely pre-empted by committees through secondment or requested "detailing" to help committee staff. It may be sufficient to have the staff member loaned to a committee to spend a large portion of each day meeting the committee's needs, but always preserving a portion of the day when the expert will be available to answer the inquiries of other legislative requestors.

Optimal Scale?   The typical size of a fully developed parliamentary library or research service seems to be about 100–200 staff (see, for example, Great Britain, Australia, Canada, India, Korea, and Japan), often comprising a varying mix of both research and reference activities. The German Bundestag has a Directorate for Reference and Research Services with a staff of 400. The U.S. Congressional Research Service is probably the largest legislative research organization, with a staff of approximately 850 – including about 525 researchers and nearly 200 librarians.

When building a new research unit (or adding research functions to an ongoing parliamentary support agency), there is considerable merit in gradual growth. For example the Hungarian unicameral Assembly plans to add 5 specialists to its Parliamentary Library to perform research tasks. This Library is a particularly hospitable home for a nascent research enterprise; it has a high–quality multilingual staff of 40 that is interdisciplinary (lawyers, economists, information technologists, as well as librarians). Poland is keeping its separate Sejm Library serving both the lower house (the Sejm) and the upper house (Senat). However, the Sejm is something of an exception to gradual growth – having launched a research and analysis unit with a staff of about 70 people in just one year – while the Senat is following the more traditional path, adding a new Research and Analysis unit with just over 30 staff members.

9.12   Relating Research and Reference Services

As touched on previously in paragraph 9.02, whether research and references services for the legislature are located in the same agency or not, they will need to be closely articulated. Members and committees will know what they want, but will be unaware of whether such a request would be classified as a research or reference inquiry. Such technical distinctions should be invisible to them. However, with two separate units handling research and reference, it will be necessary to coordinate the exchange of requests to ensure that research units are not spending an inordinate time on reference work or that reference units are not undertaking research. There is a natural (and generally functional) tendency for a legislative analyst to want to serve the client personally, whatever the need. However, this can be dysfunctional when it leads to less efficient and/or inappropriate handling of a request. Where the units are combined in the same organization, as is the case in Hungary, the U.K., and the U.S., the co-ordination tasks are simplified but still present.

With this problem in mind, it may be useful to create a central request unit to receive inquiries – especially if the research and reference units are separate. The central receiving unit would receive the requests, direct them to the appropriate organization (and person), keep track of their status, and record them in a data base. This will ensure that no request is lost, that assignments go the right organization, and that valuable user data will be collected. It also helps to ensure that all necessary data for the request is taken down, eg: deadlines for the reply, special form of presentation for the reply, etc. etc.

9.13 Building a Research Staff and Organization

The first principle of building a research capacity for the legislature is to hire high-quality staff. The second is related, namely that with respect to staffing, quality is more important than quantity. The core task of the research service – to provide information and analysis that might change the nature of the dialogue that occurs between the executive and the legislature – can be accomplished with as few as 5 of the right people. Obtaining the staff with appropriate high-level skills can occur only if the legislature appreciates the need to pay salaries that are competitive with those of the best analysts available in the ministries. For example, Senior Specialists for the Congressional Research Service have their salaries pegged by law to the highest level payable for comparable positions in the executive branch.

9.14 Organization

A high-level research staff, whether large or small, generally functions best when the organizational structure is simple and flat – with as few layers of organizational hierarchy as possible. Too many layers of review or direction will only hinder the capacity of staff to produce timely products. An overly elaborate division of labour will slow the rapid communication that must take place within the organization and among its elements while it is undertaking interdisciplinary research.

Much of the operation of the research unit, once established, will flow from informal cues rather than formal organization and procedures. Communication must take place easily from analyst to analyst – horizontally rather than up vertically through a hierarchical chain and back down again.

In terms of the internal organization of a legislative services facility, a simple structure featuring a library reference component and a research component may suffice (where these two functions are combined in one organization). As the organization grows, the research side may be elaborated by subdividing either by subject, discipline, or some combination. Because of a growing recognition that an interdisciplinary approach to policy problems is usually most effective, there should be a bias in favour of **organising by function** – combining the skills of lawyers, economists, and other social scientists in one unit to address environmental problems, another to tackle health concerns, etc.

9.15 Staff Skills

The staff of a fully-developed legislative research institution may cover a wide variety of training disciplines and subject expertise – including policy analysis, political science, history, education, agriculture, physics, engineering, environment, biology, law, economics, foreign policy, military policy and resources, computer and information science, librarianship, sociology, demography, and many others.

For a legislative research facility starting with only a few staff members, selecting which skills to acquire first is an important decision. Generically, the core skills needed to provide information and analysis for the legislature will be those of librarians, lawyers, economists, including maybe statisticians and other social scientists (historians, political scientists, sociologists). Perhaps the most important skills are those of the librarian at the outset. As an organization matures and grows, additional specialized skills may be added (science, engineering, etc.).

In the early stages of development, when combining high–level research with a large daily workload of information requests from legislators, it may be necessary to combine the skill flexibility of the librarian with the in–depth expertise of a lawyer, an economist, etc. Thus, the initial makeup of a prototype research staff might include two or three librarians and two or three specialists from other disciplines (e.g., a lawyer, an economist, and a political scientist). This is the pattern still followed by the Research Division of the U.K. House of Commons Library where a research Section will be focused on a **function**, eg Education and Social Services and consist of 4–5 subject researchers, a couple of librarians and 3–4 support staff.

Perhaps the most functional attribute to seek in hiring an individual researcher is a combination of breadth of training and perspective. This provides the subject flexibility that will prove essential when the organization is small and will require broad subject coverage by each researcher. An individual research analyst might cover two or three issue areas and serve as backup to another analyst by carrying two or three additional secondary assignments. Some doubling up of subject responsibilities is necessary if a service is to be offered during the long hours the legislature may have to sit.

As the organization grows in numbers of staff and can support more specialized backgrounds and more limited issue area assignments, it is still necessary to encourage the narrower specialties to think broadly as well as in depth. This is no simple task. The key is to provide the appropriate balance between needed disciplinary rigour and multi–causal breadth of view. Each researcher can achieve this balance to some extent through experience, training, and inculcation of research institution values. Staff can also gain this balance through participation on interdisciplinary teams.

Individual staff members for a legislative research service need to be highly trained professionals, often requiring advanced degrees. They also need to understand and support the requirement to provide balanced, objective analysis. Perhaps the quintessential personal trait is a highly intelligent curiosity or puzzle–solving mentality. Legislative researchers need to be able to express themselves well, both orally and especially in their written communication. Other desirable attributes include multi–disciplinary training or perspective, service or helping attitude, entrepreneurial skills in promoting the services of the organization with clients, clear judgment, a low tolerance for error, and a marked capacity to work under pressure with grace and humour.

Researchers must keep abreast of current events and be well informed on subjects of concern to the legislature – being particularly adept at tracking the latest status of legislation in their field of expertise. They need to understand the structure, processes, and culture both of the legislature and of the executive to be of greatest assistance to their clients.

Analysts should also continually seek to maintain and improve their subject knowledge by staying current with new information sources and in their reading of professional books and journals. They should be aware of the latest technological developments in the information industry and should be able to assess these developments for their usefulness in providing prompt and rapid information assistance to the legislature.

In their day–to–day work of providing information and analysis to the legislature, the research staff should have the ability to exercise good judgment and discretion in choosing balanced information relevant to specific requests and also be capable of exercising initiative in going beyond the normal published sources of information to answer requests. They should strive to establish contacts in as wide an area as possible, because much of the information they need will not necessarily be located in traditional books or data bases, but rather will be obtained only from knowledgeable experts in academia, governmental ministries, state or regional bodies, or independent research institutions or "think tanks" as they have come to be known. The researcher must seek to create his or her own extensive informal network of such personal sources of expertise that can be tapped through direct contact. In general it can be said that most experts are happy to cooperate with research staff to help inform the legislature.

Legislative researchers must be able to present complex material in brief understandable terms. This involves preparing highly analytical responses to legislators' questions on policy issues in terms that are easily grasped but do not sacrifice the nuances that are critical to maintaining accuracy. This is one of the most demanding requirements placed on a specialist – but one that must be learned if the products are to be useful. These written papers also represent a challenge to judgment and discretion because they must present and evaluate divergent professional opinions fairly, define and describe options briefly but in balanced fashion, and identify and discuss the consequences of making various policy choices.

9.16 The Legislative Services Environment

The work environment of a legislative research unit requires much teamwork and interdisciplinary sharing for staff to develop timely, accurate, and authoritative responses to legislative requests. This environment can be characterised as collegial and nonhierarchical, as reference and research staff work together toward their common goal of serving the legislature. Staff can be said to have a "research brokering" role between external research and information sources, on the one hand – library resources as well as contacts with professional institutions, scholars, academicians, and experts in their fields – and the legislature on the other.

The ideal mix of staff for a legislative research unit is one that contains senior professional staff from a range of disciplines who do much of the substantive work and train their younger colleagues, more junior staff who provide support to the professionals while in their learning roles, and staff with administrative, editorial, or other service-related duties.

Thus, ideally, there must be a mixture of staff who can handle legislative requests of all types, whether they require historical perspective or anticipatory planning, comparative presentations or lists of statistics, quick searches through data bases and literature or theoretical work with models and hypothetical scenarios. The needs of the individual legislature will determine the composition and numbers of staff required.

9.17   Staff Training and Development

The primary objectives of staff training and development in a legislative research institution are to increase the skills, knowledge, and abilities of the staff; to promote more efficient, effective service to the legislature; and to provide staff with opportunities for professional growth and development.

Training can be offered within the research institution by developing courses, such as orientation sessions, to familiarise staff with legislative procedures and needs. Training is also achieved by providing information on courses available at other facilities and by encouraging counselling on training and career opportunities during staff performance evaluations and at other appropriate times. One of the specialities of any in-house training should be legislative organisation and procedure. Every analyst should understand and appreciate the legislative culture in which they work, and comprehend how these facts are related to the substance of the work they do for the legislature.

Because it is important for staff to stay abreast of developments in their subject specialisations, they should be encouraged to participate in their respective professional associations and to attend and present papers at national and international conferences. Their personal enrichment by being actively engaged in these endeavours will add to the contributions they bring to the legislative service.

It may be useful for professional development to encourage staff exchanges for limited time periods of one to six months with other government agencies or the research institutions of other nations. These exchanges can offer new ideas and approaches to legislative research staff, while forging helpful personal links to the institutions of other nations that can facilitate informational exchange between legislatures.

9.18 Managing Time and Tasks: The Management–Staff Interface

The unique problems of a legislative research service – with requisites of timeliness, accuracy, objectiveness, balance, nonpartisanship, and confidentiality – often require creative solutions and responses. Both managers and staff of legislative research institutions must be aware of deadlines, priorities, and both the strengths and weaknesses of the staff in meeting legislative requests. The team approach can bring a variety of skills to a task and help alleviate any perceived lack of adequate strengths to meet a request goal. Management and staff thus work together to bring the best expertise to bear on a particular legislative request within time and cost constraints.

A consultative management approach, in which management and staff are partners in change, is often helpful in identifying potential problems, finding joint solutions, and sharing information about results. This management approach is especially beneficial in a research environment because it can ensure engagement of the creative energy and ideas of all staff in implementing operational changes as an institution evolves, and can encourage staff to enrich the quality of their work environment and contribute to the goals of the research institution.

CHAPTER 10

RESEARCH : SERVICES OF RESEARCH AND ANALYSIS
IN A LEGISLATIVE ENVIRONMENT

10.01 **Introduction**

There is an important distinction to be made between the nature of research services and that of reference services. (See also para 10.10 below). The provision of reference services frequently entails searching out materials on a given subject and examining their relevance to the question asked; but the evaluation process stops there, with selected materials being passed on to the requestor for further study and evaluation. In performing legislative research, however, the analyst completes the evaluation process and applies the assessment of the data in the creation of a new information product.

10.02 A number of the smaller libraries have one or more staff members who are designated as research staff, but this title is usually a misnomer in the analytical sense. In the context set forth in the preceding paragraph, these staff are responsible for the reference work which involves ferreting out pertinent source materials and evaluating their relevance to the type of information request most frequently made by Members, which is: "Please get me information on [one or another topic of legislative debate]."

10.03 The work performed by research analysts certainly begins with a search for and evaluation of relevant data; but beyond that, the analyst must explain in cogent terms, either in an oral brief or in a written report, why the information is relevant and how it affects one or another possible policy option. The written document may take one of several forms. It may be a one to two page summary or a briefing note of five to ten pages. Background studies of significant issues, usually written for general distribution to all Members, tend to run considerably longer although there is no established standard length for such documents. In some cases, particularly with respect to in–depth analyses of major national policy issues, the research report may take the form of a monograph possibly of several hundred pages. The research branch of some legislatures, for example that of the U.S. Congress and the Parliament of Turkey, also publish periodic journals to which the research analysts, and in some cases Members, contribute scholarly articles on topics of high legislative interest. The majority of the work however will be shorter reports targeted to the requests of specific Members but usually intended for distribution to all interested Members and produced on a very rapid turn around.

10.04   Given that the primary function of a legislature is law–making, legal research is of paramount importance. The record of legislation as it passes through the legislative process, and references to its antecedents in the case of amending legislation, is generally referred to as a legislative history. The preparation of legislative histories, digests or summaries of the salient features of bills, and even clause by clause comparisons of the language in an existing statute with that of proposed amending legislation are routine tasks performed either by the legal research staff in a very large service, or specialists in the subject being legislated about in medium sized services. The indexing and analysis of current legislation may be the responsibility of part of the library or information service as described in Chapter 13.

10.05   Mention was made earlier (see 9.03) of the fact that the research staff may, and generally do, perform a substantial amount of work in support of the legislative business of standing and special committees. In addition, in the most developed services they are sometimes assigned to accompany committees or subcommittees on foreign study tours as expert advisors. To prepare Members to go on foreign tours, briefing booklets are sometimes produced. The booklets present summary information on the socio–political culture, economy, and government of the country or countries to be visited, highlighting points of significant interests and concerns in bilateral relations. They may also include maps and relevant statistical tables, such as current figures on imports and exports. Essentially, however, they are meant to set out the salient facts regarding the topic(s) to be discussed with foreign officials during the course of the tour. Where available, biographical information on the persons to be met would also be included.

10.06 The type of research undertaken by legislative research services is generally of a secondary or tertiary nature. That is to say, it involves, as a rule, the synthesis and analysis of data collected and published by other individuals and institutions rather than that obtained through direct field study or personal observation and experimentation. However, it involves much more than simply describing the findings of others. The strengths and weaknesses of arguments for and against an existing or a proposed policy and the identification and assessment of various possible alternatives must be presented in a dispassionate and balanced analytical manner so as not to favour one or another partisan faction in the legislature. It is for the legislators themselves to make the relevant value judgments on behalf of their respective constituencies and to argue the facts of a matter in terms of any political manifesto or goal.

In addition to fulfilling the mandate for impartiality, research staff must also respect the confidentiality of requests made by individual Members and ensure that any tailored research product is responsive to the Member's inquiry. In the process of taking in the requests, therefore, it is important that pertinent questions are asked so that the parameters of the research to be undertaken are clearly defined at the outset. For internal management purposes, such as meeting institutional reporting requirements and preparing budget justifications, some appropriate form of inquiry control, along with the related record keeping of workload statistics and the like, needs to be maintained.

10.07 Quality control over the research output in a political institution is a rather critical concern. It is difficult at best for any individual to be truly objective about issues which, by virtue of their being the subject of political and legal debate, are inherently controversial. Furthermore, fairly rigorous conformity to the requisite standards of relevance, accuracy, and substantive merit in the research work must be sustained. However, these factors must be balanced against the other crucial priority of getting work out in the time-frame in which Members need the information. The process of reviewing the work at various levels (i.e. peer review, supervisory review, managerial review) needs to be carefully considered, and whatever procedure is adopted should be consistently followed so that it is perceived throughout the constitution as reliable thorough and fair.

10.08 As was stated earlier, a certain portion of the research work in a legislature is presented orally. Because of the time pressure put on Members as a result of the communications revolution of recent decades, telephones, television, fax etc, this is a quickly growing area of work for research staff. It requires additional talents, especially in terms of clarity and speed of thinking and expression, to the traditional talent of being a good researcher. This work may take the form of informal consultations or discussions with individual Members as well as more formal briefings for committees or other groups of Members. In the former instance, there may be no prior specific preparation undertaken at all. The latter case will usually entail the preparation of at least an outline of main points or notes to be referred to, perhaps some charts or diagrams, and possibly a handout of some sort. Obviously , these oral presentations require not only a reasonable articulateness but also considerable subject knowledge and a sound sense of professional and political judgment. These factors need to be taken into account in the recruitment, selection, and promotion of research staff.

10.09 The research staff can play a vital role in Member education programmes (see 7.08) and in the production of audiovisual aids on substantive issues (see 7.10). These are essentially just specialised forms of the oral presentation of research studies, but they can be very effective means of information dissemination to Members. As a general characteristic, politicians would much rather listen to and participate in discussions of important public issues than read about them. Even those who are inclined to read, find that they have very little time for quiet, thoughtful study. For those Members of developing countries who are unable to read, the oral tradition is their only means of gathering information and exchanging ideas. Seminars and audio visual programmes are innovative, action-orientated endeavours and, because of this, convey a sense of organisational dynamism to which Members tend to respond favourably. In sum, then,

Audiovisual Media and other types of oral presentation ought to be utilised to the fullest extent possible in developing or enhancing legislative research services.

10.10 Parliamentary Research: Some Important Distinctions

As already indicated, research and analysis for a legislative body is clearly different from reference work. In research, there is a need for specialisation and subject expertise that goes well beyond what is expected in reference work. Moreover, the demands transcend facts and information to include deeper insights into potential causes of social problems and approaches to their solution.

Yet the term "research" in a parliamentary setting also has far different connotations than it has in academia. Academic research tends to convey notions of pure research, or long-lasting endeavours to discover truth and fundamental relationships in society for the purpose of advancing knowledge and understanding. Research for a legislature is more applied in nature, seeking to draw on existing knowledge and apply it to the understanding and solution of immanent concrete problems. It is knowledge sought for a more specific and limited purpose. In many ways, the term "research" should probably always have a modifier attached to it when used in a legislative setting. Policy research or policy analysis are technically more descriptive of the real activity when applied to a legislature.

A highly useful concept to apply to the activities of a legislative research analyst, or research officer as they are known in some parliamentary libraries already mentioned in paragraph 9.16 above, is to envision their role as one of being a "broker" of information – constantly scanning the world of outside knowledge for those concepts and findings that will shed light on the nature of public policy problems and then recasting those concepts into terms and frameworks that can be more readily used in the legislature. The **"research broker"** is a nexus for bringing together the world of ideas and the world of action. The broker is comfortable in both worlds and is "bi-lingual," that is, able to speak the languages of both research and policy fluently. As such he or she is translator, interpreter, and alchemist – being capable of seeing policy relevance in ideas that the research world itself might have missed and then reframing those concepts into usable solutions to policy problems. Often without this broker, the ideas useful in search of problems and the problems in need of solution might never be brought together. The concept of research broker also reflects the fact that time is limited for the legislative analyst, and that the search for other people's ideas as a time–saving device is not only efficient (ensuring that the wheel only gets invented once), but constructive in bridging gaps between those who know and those who need to know because they must act (the legislators). In all these activities, the broker must understand that his or her role is that of agent – assisting the legislature in obtaining and using information needed to make sound public policy.

Because of its practical orientation, policy research or analysis is also more concerned with concrete implementation concerns and administrative feasibility than is ordinary research. Political constraints are also brought from the periphery of the discussion to play a more central role in analysis than in more academic undertakings.

Another important distinction about legislative research is its greater tendency to be interdisciplinary in nature. Academic departments in universities are almost universally devoted to a single method of inquiry or discipline. Economics departments train economists, who then seek appropriate problems to which they can apply their economic analysis skills. Law schools and lawyers do the same. Yet analysis of public policy problems requires the combined skills of subject experts, lawyers, economists, etc.

The issue of trade policy provides a useful concrete example. It is possible to focus only on the economic dimension of trade – in which case the long–term benefits of free trade often drive the analysis inexorably to undervalue the importance of short–term labour adjustment problems as workers lose their jobs and politicians take up the cause of adjustment assistance or even protection. To ignore this political reality risks consigning analysis to irrelevance and subjecting the judgment of the research organisation to attack (and possibly its budget as well). Yet to dwell only on the political concerns of trade threatens to descend into beggar–thy–neighbour

64

protectionism and the sacrifice of significant long–term benefits to all. Effective analysis of trade policy must therefore involve economics, politics, legal exploration of intellectual property rights, science policy for research and development, and appropriate consideration of international and foreign policy dimensions.

Finally, a few closing words about terminology and the unique perspective of this chapter, which tends to set it apart from the other more general chapters in this volume. This chapter on research sets forth principles that are primarily applicable to larger parliamentary libraries and research centres, and takes a more expansive view of what constitutes "research," which only a few parliamentary libraries presently incorporate in their entirety in their products and services. Most of this chapter describes the perspective of the U.S. Congressional Research Service (CRS) as it strives to meet the needs of a large complex legislature representing 250 million people, in an overall system often characterised by competition between the separate institutions for legislative and the executive functions. While only the larger libraries will employ many of the approaches and principles espoused in this chapter, they may be useful as checkpoints for any parliamentary information provider to view as a "cafeteria" of choices that are available for careful adaptation to their unique circumstances. In that regard, it is appropriate to note that smaller parliamentary libraries may have one or more people called "research officers," even though they often perform reference work either because of time constraints or more limited specialised training. While this may appear to be a misuse of terms in some technical sense, it is not a serious concern. Even some of the larger parliamentary libraries will have most of their resources engaged in reference work with only a few specialists actually engaging in research (for example, the Korean Parliamentary Library has a staff of more than 200, but only about a dozen are estimated to be doing research work). In the end, terms are not terribly important, as long as people understand the meaning of those terms in the local context.

10.11 The Range of Research Activities for the Legislature

As suggested above (10.10), and in the Introduction to this Chapter (10.01) the term research covers a wide range of activity. At one end of the continuum, there is a an overlap of activities that might be characterised as either research or reference. The search for specific facts falls into this area. Certainly some fact gathering is reference activity; however, when specialised knowledge is required to isolate data that are analytically meaningful, one has made the leap to research. For example, under what circumstances is it more appropriate to use gross domestic product (GDP) rather than net domestic product? If the context of the inquiry makes it clear that the decision is unambiguous for using GDP, then it is a reference inquiry. If you need the specialised skills and judgment of an economist to answer whether net domestic product is more meaningful in the context of the inquiry, you have gravitated to the low end of the research enterprise.

The next level of activity on the research continuum is that of locating and synthesising articles and expert opinions that identify problems on the public policy agenda. Related tasks at this level include summarising what others have said about the causes of the problem and possible solutions. Adding a pro–con analysis of the options presented by others, or offering a comparison and contrast of the analyses of others may constitute further movement along the continuum. Still higher levels of analysis include offering data that illuminate causal linkages and/or additional choices for action not suggested in the literature but that follow reasonably from the facts and knowledge of the issue at hand. Both these steps enhance the information available to the decisionmakers, but do not yet break new ground analytically.

Requiring more expert knowledge – and a great deal more time – is the step involving the gathering of isolated primary data that highlight the nature, scale, and severity of a public policy problem. This represents the beginning of original problem solving and may even become a set of indicators for analysing, understanding, and tracking a particular issue in a new light. At some point, this level of research has the potential of leading to new findings about the causes of problems or novel attempts at their solution. Often at this point complex mathematical procedures to determine the degree variables are covered or to help resolve the question of chance or causality are brought into play. Whatever the complexity of tool used, the results are written about or displayed in clear, understandable terms for easy digestion by the non-technical legislator.

One of the highest levels of research and analysis for a legislature is that of tracing the effects or implications of policy options before they are implemented. This often requires the development of computer simulation models in order to test the possible effects of actions under different possible conditions or assumptions. The process of developing a simulation model tests the highest skills of the researcher. It requires identification of key factors that influence the activity under consideration, as well as the stipulation of likely direction and degrees of relationship between independent and dependent variables – which is another way of saying describing **causal** relationships. Clearly, the researcher must have achieved a profound understanding of the policy problem if he or she is able to say something meaningful about likely causes of the problem and then go on to trace the possible effects of alternative solutions based on his/her understanding of the interaction of forces surrounding the problem. Reaching this level of analysis is also a way to test the degree of understanding of the problem and to impose structure on one's knowledge, because it requires the quantitative explication of relationships that can otherwise be left vague or qualitative in nature using other less demanding methods. It also enables one to test the accuracy of those presumed relationships by running the model to determine how well it replicates reality – i.e., can the researcher use the model to recreate the current situation with a high degree of accuracy? If the present state cannot be replicated, then little meaningful information can be gathered by moving into the projection period. It is of interest in the context of this paragraph that the recently established Macroeconomic Working Group established by the correspondents of the European Centre for Parliamentary Research and Documentation, consisting of most of the legislative libraries and information services of European Parliaments has quickly become one of the most active of the Centre's working groups.

In effect, this description of the levels of research has traced the classical definition of policy analysis – identifying the underlying causes of a policy problem in a way that enables the policymaker to focus on genuine solutions rather than being distracted by more obvious symptoms; offering alternative choices for solving or ameliorating the problem; and tracing the likely impacts or effects of these various possible actions **before** they are taken so that the legislator can make a truly reasoned choice. The only missing step from textbook definitions of policy analysis is that of making recommendations. As discussed in chapter 9, making recommendations requires the analyst to make value judgments that are more appropriately reserved to the elected legislator. The legislative researcher must stop short of this step, being satisfied with assisting the legislator by giving him or her the raw materials for making a wise choice, but leaving the actual choice – which involves the assessment of the political and moral imperatives – to the person(s) elected to make binding value choices for the rest of society.

10.12 Kinds of Research Products and Services

The forms of products and services depend on the size of the legislative service agency and its budget. The types of response can vary from simple informative products and services offered by a small staff to more sophisticated products and services provided by a large multidisciplinary staff with access to computerised data bases. Responses to legislative inquiries can be oral or written. They can range from quick responses via telephone "hotline" to an in–depth policy analysis requiring days or months to prepare.

A multitude of analytical written products can be prepared to address issues of legislative interest: analytical reports defining issues and analysing causes and alternative proposed solutions (ranging from a few to several hundred pages, depending on the complexity of the topic), legal analysis, digests of bills and legislation, bill comparisons, legislative histories, materials for use in drafting speeches, compilations of facts and statistics, and information packets by subject area.

Information services can take the form of bibliographic materials, including searches of products available and other public policy literature. Other services might include copies of specific items, such as journal or newspaper excerpts or clippings, scientific or technical reports, legal or government documents, books borrowed from a library's collections, photocopies of requested material, or compilations of products and articles on current topics. Reading rooms might be provided where reference services are offered, if space permits.

Translation and assistance with correspondence in foreign languages can also be part of the range of services offered to legislators.

Other services, such as in-person consultations, can be helpful to the busy legislator with little time for reading, as might professional development programs for legislative members and their staff - including seminars and workshops on specific topics of policy interest or legislative institutes on parliamentary procedures and operations. Access to computer data bases, video and audio tapes, and other products might be offered to enhance legislative services, where funds and technology are available.

While the kinds of research services and products are theoretically infinite in number, it is possible to reduce this potentially limitless variety into some meaningful categories. For example, one such classification might be to sort by media: written products, oral presentations or briefings, and audio or video services (including the use of computer data bases). Within each category, a number of generic products might be identified. This approach has the advantage of being comparative while not exhaustive or too lengthy.

10.13 Written Products

Written products are the backbone of a legislative research organisation. Even when initial information is provided orally, Members of Parliament or their staff nearly always wish to carry away something that they can read for greater depth or to refresh their memory of the conversation. Written products can also be used as "workload managers" by building an inventory of useful products that can be taken quickly from the shelf when needed to meet information requirements as they arise. Generically, written products can be reduced to a few basic categories:

–   **Brief legal reports**, including reports on the status of major bills before the legislature, summary descriptions of legislation, legal analysis of major legislation, and legislative histories of major enactments of the legislature. This category is the starting point for any legislative research group, and should be as comprehensive as resources permit. For example, CRS provides a digest of *all legislation* before the Congress (which, in the case of the 102d Congress involved 12,018 items of legislation through the end of calendar year 1992), and maintains this in a data base both on–line in a computerised access system, and soon to be available in a CD–ROM version to replace the old printed form formerly published quarterly.

–   **Bibliographies**, which do not require extensive specialised resources, or new writing by a limited parliamentary library staff, but which can be used to provide background information on issues. Some skill and judgment must be exercised in selecting sources, to keep the bibliography from becoming too voluminous or one–sided. Care should be exercised to provide a balanced selection of readings, because objectivity is a goal to be pursued in all forms of response. This form of response might also be used by any library or research service as interim responses on fast–breaking issues, until some more targeted response can be written. There are also some issues that are so controversial that the bibliography may be the safest form of response. The most useful bibliography is the **annotated bibliography**, which provides a summary description of what is to be found in each of the major references.

–   **Background papers**, which are written by the staff to describe a program, problem, or issue – but which do not go very deeply into analysis or actions that might be taken to alleviate the problem. These are also very popular as workload managers both for Members and staff of the legislature for their own use, and for distribution to their constituents to broaden public understanding or to respond to public inquiries. These background papers can be lengthy or brief, depending upon the need. However, if the background paper is more than three or four pages, it should contain a one-page summary for easy digestion by busy readers. A very handy variant of this report form is the one- or two-page factsheet, which is easy to read and carries a high volume of information for the busy legislator.

– **Memoranda and other personalised responses** are often extremely valuable because they are focused specifically on the question being asked by a Member of Parliament or staff. The other products mentioned in this section are usually prepared for general distribution, and tend to be more discursive in nature. The memorandum, because it addresses a specific question, tends to be briefer and more direct. It is also more likely to be confidential, intended for the specific and personal use of the requester. In some legislative services, this might take the form of a personal and therefore confidential letter to the Member raising the issue.

– **Option papers**, describing a legislative issue, but moving beyond that stage to provide an array of alternative actions that mitigate the problem – as well as analysing the options as to their impacts and relative effectiveness in dealing with the problem. Option papers may also assess the risks of unintended consequences or potentially dire results that may attend one or more options.

– **Special products** can be created from these generic examples that can meet a variety of purposes. For example, two kinds of written products have proven extremely useful to CRS in meeting a high volume of requests. The first such product is an *Issue Brief*. CRS maintains approximately 350 Issue Briefs on topics of current legislative interest to the U.S. Congress. Each of these briefs is 15 pages or less, provides an analysis of the issue, traces legislative activity and other sources of information, and has a one-page summary at the beginning for easy use. These briefs are kept current as legislative issues develop and are available on-line in a computer data base immediately accessible in Member offices as well as in hard copy. They are very popular, and have become the flagship of the CRS product line. The second of these special products are *Info Packs* which are collections of materials most consistently in demand in order to respond to questions raised by constituents of Members of Congress. These collections may include clippings and other products produced by others for fast–breaking issues when the press of time makes it impossible for the research service to create a custom product for immediate use. They may be made available for browsing and personal pick–up for easy accessibility. *Issue Briefs* and *Info Packs* are used in responding to more than half of the inquiries made to CRS, and make off–the–shelf material available very quickly, while also protecting the research staff from having to divert their attention from more longer–range, more in–depth pursuits to handle current workload. Smaller research staffs may make use of these principles by maintaining fewer numbers of shorter briefs or *Info Packs*. Even 5–10 Issue Briefs can make a difference in the service rendered to a legislature, its perception of research services, and the ability to carve out some time for longer–term issue development.

10.14 Other Research Products and Services

While written products are the backbone of the legislative research product line, the lifeblood may be **oral communication and in–person briefings**. In a legislative setting, the spoken word is often the fastest, most targeted, mobile, and preferred form of communication. The medium for such expression may be a telephone call for a specific fact needed in floor debate immediately, or a more leisurely briefing of a Member of Parliament on a topic of current interest. The face–to–face setting makes it possible for the Member or staff aide to ask questions, probe for additional material, assess the validity and confidence range of more speculative analyses, and test understanding and meaning while the expert is still present. When this activity takes place in legislative chambers, awaiting a scheduled vote or debate, it often means that the researcher carries whatever information is needed in his or her head rather than a briefcase. The Member may start on one line of questioning, but quickly skip to another – one for which the briefer has no available materials and must rely on what is currently recalled. The oral dimension of the legislative setting places an added responsibility on the researcher to be adept at both written and oral communication. Not all thoughtful researchers are equally competent at "thinking on their feet," but this is a dimension of their professional development that must be cultivated and improved. It requires more than a glib tongue, but immense judgment in selecting the relevant facts, and their order of presentation –all in an instant.

A time deficit also contributes to the growing popularity of **audio and video products.** Cassette tapes can be created on topics of interest to be played at the convenience of the legislator or staffer – typically while travelling to or from the parliament. In the same spirit, an important seminar can be videotaped and replayed for the busy Member who was unable to attend.

Parliaments often look to their staff of experts to provide **training** in their areas of expertise to Members' personal staff and occasionally Members as well. In the United States, for example, CRS conducts training programs on legislative organisation and procedures, on how to conduct legislative research, on sources of information and how to use them, and on a variety of other processes and policy areas to literally thousands of congressional staff each year. This provides a direct service to the individual in enhancing their skills, while also making the parliament itself more effective. Training also reduces CRS workload by answering frequently asked questions in a group setting, and providing tools that others can use to answer their own questions.

10.15 **Quality Control**

Legislative bodies in open democratic societies are often besieged by advocates pressing their particular needs and biased views. The reference and research facility for a legislature must establish high standards in order to provide objective, nonpartisan analysis that can be trusted and used by all parties. That is the path chosen by the United States, as well as the British, German, Australian, Canadian, and Indian legislative libraries, among others.

Although objective analysis is the norm for the legislative research agency, making policy recommendations is clearly inappropriate. The role of the research staff is to analyse, compare, and contrast alternatives; the value choices inherent in making recommendations are the exclusive province of the elected legislator.

Other standards for a legislative research facility, besides objectivity, are accuracy and authoritativeness, timeliness, clarity, discretion and confidentiality – all values to be upheld in a legislative environment where legislators rely on the knowledge, products, and services of the research unit. Because the legislator is often a nonspecialist, it is the responsibility of the research staff to work exclusively for the legislature in order to focus on its information needs; to present even the most technical material in clear, accurate, and understandable terms; and to present the information in a timely manner, with confidentiality if needed. Legislators need to rely on these high standards of the research support in order to make informed decisions on matters that may bind society with the force of law.

Peer review and policy review by the staff of a research facility are the hallmarks of successful products and services. The more thoroughly considered and multidisciplinary the research approach, with pros and cons presented in a balanced discussion, the more useful are the results to the legislator.

10.16 Committee Support

Committee support, referred to at 10.05 above, is an important part of legislative services. Assistance to ensure continuous liaison with committees and their work can include help with the formulation, analysis, and evaluation of legislative proposals, as well as presentation of expert testimony, preparation of briefing books, and participation in committee investigative delegations. Legislative research staff are available to work closely with committees during all stages of the legislative process, and can help with committee planning and scheduling at the beginning of legislative sessions. Research staff can meet with committees to discuss subject and policy areas of concern to them. Committees can receive the same research, analysis, and information support that is provided to individual legislative member offices.

10.17 Dissemination and Communication

There can be many avenues of communication between legislators and the legislative research unit – methods of placing legislative requests and methods of disseminating information. Simple information inquiries from legislators are often received via telephone hotline or a products telephone line when specific reference items are needed. Requests for policy analysis or other more detailed inquiries can be made by a phone call, followed by a meeting or a letter. Other means of sending requests include facsimile communication and electronic mail where the technology is feasible, and in-person visits by the legislator to the research facility where distance is not a problem.

In a large and developed system, the dissemination of information can occur through regular, generally monthly, mailings of such materials as product listings, perhaps a policy analysis journal focusing on issues before the legislature, announcements of issue-specific seminars, workshops, and similar events. Training programs can be offered to familiarise new members with legislative procedures, and other programs can be tailored to the needs of legislative staff.

Other dissemination may take place through specially prepared, perhaps daily recorded messages of changes in economic or demographic statistics, available to legislators by telephone. Where possible, audio or visual tapes may be available, often by loan, to supplement or enhance issues of interest for legislators who have little time to read prepared documents.

10.18 Automation for Increased Speed and Breadth of Service

A legislative research unit strives to meet the information and research needs of the legislature with the most effective information systems and services. The challenge is to make the best use of information technology within the limits of the resources available in a field of constant, rapid change.

Up–to–date information technology is essential to the work of legislative research facilities, particularly those that serve large legislative bodies. It can provide central tools for the most fundamental tasks – computers to prepare reports and memoranda, for example, and optical disk technology to produce copies of public policy literature requested by legislative members and staff. This technology can extend the knowledge of the reference and research unit by providing access through data bases and communications systems to information in other regions and, increasingly, throughout the world. Some of this technology makes it possible for researchers to do forecasting and modelling accurately and quickly, and to have access to increased data files and opinion polls, etc. Such tools enable the research staff to keep pace with the changing needs of legislators as they face the growing complexity of issues and increased need for quality information delivered within a short timeframe

10.18   Legislative Needs Assessment and Planning for the Future

One way to provide a legislature with what it requires is to develop an ability to look ahead and anticipate needs and issues. If analysis is to be useful, it must be ready *before* legislators have made up their minds, put their names on bills, and taken a vote. Thus early availability of information, selectively chosen with foresight, improves the quality and appropriateness of its use by the legislator. Yet the ability of a research unit to operate at this level is dependent on anticipatory strategies and active assessments of both substantive and institutional needs.

Although there is an infinite variety of techniques for assessing the changing needs of a legislature, some have proven useful in forecasting the issues that come before a legislature such as the U.S. Congress. By drawing on the intelligence from working closely with the legislative process, a legislative research unit can anticipate the issues likely to be ready for consideration during a session. Each year, for instance, as part of a major issue planning system, legislative analysts and their managers can seek to ensure focus and provide sufficient time in advance to conduct in–depth research (and model-building, where appropriate and when resources permit), to employ comprehensive interdisciplinary approaches rather than segmented single-view assessments, and to deploy that analysis when it is needed. Specific research teams may be formed for each major issue and special products may be developed as part of this issue planning and tracking system.

Besides anticipating substantive issues to track in order to assist the legislature, a research unit must continually assess how well its current products and services are meeting needs, what new ones may be more effective in addressing emerging legislative requirements, and whether changes are needed in form, timing, or site of services. Systematic scanning of the policy environment by the research unit may yield problems, trends, and developments that determine the environment for legislative decisions. Continuous liaison with legislative committees helps ensure that analysis is on target and is used in the legislative process. Periodic management "retreats" for the research unit staff are helpful in focusing on research directions and goals.

Needs assessment is a demanding task that increases workload and entails an element of risk. Yet it is necessary if a research unit is to offer the most effective assistance to the legislature.

SPECIAL SERVICES FOR LEGISLATORS

Introduction

In the first ten chapters of *Guidelines for Legislative Libraries*, much emphasis has been placed on Members' need for current information, the importance of modern information technology in aiding legislators and the Parliament's own work as part of the information sources for Members. Part IV discusses these aspects of the work of legislative libraries as distinctive services which are likely to be of assistance to users and describes specific activities in the Norwegian Parliament in Oslo (Chapter 11) and the UK Parliament at Westminster (Chapter 13). In addition, there is a general chapter on do's and don't's when considering Information Technology in particular in the context of a legislature.

CHAPTER 11

MEDIATING NEWS AND PUBLIC OPINION TO MEMBERS OF PARLIAMENT

11.01 Introduction

The need for Members of Parliament to be informed about recent news and public opinion, is obvious. This an be achieved through various means, and the purpose here is to examine some of them, drawing on experience from the Library of the Norwegian Parliament.

The point of departure is that such mediating is related to a <u>horizontal</u> as well as a <u>vertical</u> dimension. The former implies specifically that news and public opinion are mediated along a dimension from informal <u>direct contact</u> via persons and interest groups at one end, through traditional means like <u>newspapers</u> and <u>broadcasting</u> to the more advanced means of <u>news indexing</u> – often by the use of databases – at the other. The vertical dimension indicates that news and public opinion can originate on various <u>levels;</u> that is <u>locally</u>, <u>nationally</u> and <u>internationally</u>. These two dimensions are illustrated in the figure below, indicating a certain relationship between the two as well.

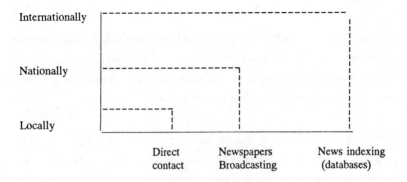

My point of departure when looking more closely at the mediating of news and public opinion for MPs, will be these two dimensions. More precisely I relate the means of mediating to the various levels on which news and public opinion originate. In so doing it also seems natural to make a certain distinction between news and public opinion, even though they are related and equally important to the parliamentarian. Finally, a distinction between "today's news" and what I will call "yesterday's news", is relevant as well.

Even though this is usually not included in the group of media, and does not involve the parliamentary library, direct contact between parliamentarians and both persons and interest groups is worth mentioning. It is such direct and regular contact that helps the MPs to keep informed, primarily of course on public opinion and debate, and most often on issues originating locally, that is in his own constituency. Most issues dealt with in that fashion by the parliamentarian relate specifically to the day-to-day problems of ordinary people.

In the Norwegian Parliament – and I will assume this is true for many parliaments – there is a long tradition of people being able to convey their interests and opinions directly to MPs. Likewise there is a tradition of organizations and interest groups presenting petitions and meeting with Parliamentary committees to express their views.

11.02 Newspapers

The reading of newspapers, local, national and to a certain extent foreign, constitutes an important part of an MP's day. Being at all times informed on the latest events, both in his own constituency, as well as at national level, and on the inter-national scene, is obviously expected of Members of Parliament.

With the publication of more than 150 newspapers and a population of 4 million people, Norway can justifiably claim to be a big producer of newspapers. The papers will of course vary in size and frequency. While some are dailies, others come 2 to 5 times a week; and while some bring primarily local news, others will be more national and international in character.

The flow of national newspapers will naturally be reflected in a parliamentary library; more precisely by being made available in the library's reading room. In order also to meet the need among parliamentarians to keep informed on foreign affairs, newspapers from other countries must be made available in the reading room as well. In the Library of the Norwegian Parliament 42 foreign newspapers are subscribed to at the moment.

In other words, the MPs should, in the parliamentary library's reading room, be able to read the local news from his own constituency, the national newspapers, as well as the larger and more important foreign ones. That means newspapers should be available at all three levels. He may not be allowed to take the papers out of the reading room, but should have easy access to a photo-coping machine close by to take all the copies he needs.

As for the actual handling of newspapers in the library, I will say a few words about the distinction made initially between "today's news" and "yesterday's news". Let me start by saying the library will of course not be the only place in a parliament where Members can get hold of newspapers. Not only do Members themselves receive a fair number directly in their mail, but, as in the Norwegian Parliament, there may also be a special reading room centrally located in the building with newspapers and magazines.

Even though the national newspapers can be found elsewhere in the legislature, and the MPs receive these as well as their local newspaper sent directly to their office, the library will usually have the largest and most systematic collection, and in particular, be the only place where newspapers are kept systematically and stored. The library will thus be the only place able to answer requests for "yesterday's news". And such requests are frequently made – the reason being that even though the news as such is well known when published, the ensuing commentaries, statements or interviews will continue to be of interest.

In other words, even though the main purpose of news media is to mediate the latest events, they also have a role to play when news is no longer new, precisely because parliamentarians may need to clarify comments or statements made in relation to the news by a political adversary or a fellow party member. Thus, not only to make available today's newspapers but also to put some effort into the keeping of this material, is an important task for a parliamentary library.

Of the 139 Norwegian newspapers received in the Library of the Norwegian Parliament, around 30 are permanently stored; from the 1970s on microfilm. The period for which others are kept varies from 2–3 months to a couple of years. This means that a certain effort goes into making "yesterday's news" available to the user, but our experience is that it is well worth while. Microfilming reduces the space problem and means that this material, rather than being kept in remote storage rooms, can be more readily accessible.

As no indexing is done in the library of newspaper articles, finding the right issue requires that the enquirer should be fairly precise in indicating the date the news was published. As most newspapers do their own indexing, however, the library will make use of these when necessary. Such indexing is increasingly done in databases, and the retrieval of material from newspapers in the future will become much easier, and the need for storage will be reduced.

A possible service to MPs regarding newspaper material, is a daily clipping service on issues of particular interest. This is no doubt a time consuming task for a library, but it may seem worth while. It helps keep the library informed on issues on the political agenda and it helps integrate the library services into the current work of parliament. At present such a service is not offered by the Library of the Norwegian Parliament. Rather the various party secretariats do the clipping for their respective Members. As this, no doubt, means a duplication of clippings, the idea has been put forward that the library should take over this service. Considering the positive aspects indicated above, this may therefore be a service offered by the library in the future.

11.03 Broadcasting

Leaving the newspapers, I now turn to another important news media, namely radio and television. Dealing with this media I will also describe a special service offered by the Library of the Norwegian Parliament regarding programmes on radio and television, more precisely the service of the library's "mediatek".

Through regular programmes on current events including commentaries and interviews, as well as debate and discussion programmes, radio and television are important mediators of both news and public opinion.

In the Norwegian Parliament all Members have access in their office to the two national radio stations and to a television set where they can watch all channels available in the Oslo area.

Radio and television is also installed in the library and constitutes the basis for the library's "mediatek". As indicated above, I will spend some time presenting the kind of service it offers to MPs in the Norwegian Parliament. This service was originally requested by the MPs themselves, and as it is highly appreciated, it may be an idea for other parliamentary libraries as well.

The "mediatek", in addition to being a room where MPs may hear or see programmes on radio or television, it is also the place where programmes from these media are recorded on tapes and on video and stored for two months. This means that what was said earlier about the need to make available "yesterday's news" from newspapers, goes for radio and television programmes as well. Thus, by this recording, the library is able to respond to a need to listen to or view "yesterday's news" programmes, as well as debates and discussions, indicating public opinion on various issues.

The most recent use of the "mediatek" is to make written survey of the morning news headlines and to send this directly to the various party secretariats and standing committees. Such a service was initially requested by one of the party secretariat, but was offered to others as well, and is now a highly appreciated service undertaken by the library every morning.

The service of supplying MPs with recordings of programmes from radio and television on a regular basis, goes back to 1972. As indicated above, it was established in response to the parliamentarians' wish to be able to hear, and possibly get transcripts of programmes, both newsreporting and commentaries, but also debates and discussions on radio and television. These were programmes that they either had not been able to hear when they were transmitted or they had been made aware of afterwards. To offer this service seemed an appropriate task for the library, and the equipment for recording, as well as the way in which the service has been executed, has gradually become more and more sophisticated and useful, benefitting from technological advances and improved methods.

While the tapes initially were obtained from outside the library equipment has now been acquired so the library can make the recordings direct. This means that a copy of the tape or the video can be provided soon after a programme has been broadcast, the next day at the latest.

Recordings are made from the two national radio stations of certain programmes automatically; these include all news programmes, reports, discussion programmes and so on. As for the national television channel, the recordings cover most of the programmes shown. At the moment there is only one official television station in Norway.

When applying for a certain programme on radio or television, the MP may either listen to or watch the programme in the "mediatek", or he may get a copy, that is a cassette or a video sent to his office. Initially a transcript of a programme was provided by the library, but as a written version is a very time consuming service and as the MPs gradually got cassette and video equipment in their own offices, a cassette or video means a much quicker service. If especially asked for and if the programme is not too long, a transcript may, however, still be provided.

Let me also mention that when a transcript of a radio or television programme is provided, a copy is kept and registered in the library. In the short term this is useful because more than one request is likely to come for the same programme, and also because some of the material may constitute an important source in future reference work. The requests are steadily increasing, and this is especially true when certain issues are the subject of hot debate between the political parties or are otherwise reflected in public discussion. Likewise an increase can be seen prior to an election. This reflects of course, what was indicated initially, namely that parliamentarians need to keep informed concerning issues high on the political agenda. Their need to use the "mediatek" in order to achieve this is linked to their special occupation. Being a Member of Parliament means frequent meetings and much travelling, which in turn means that they are not always able to listen to or watch programmes on radio or television which are beneficial or essential to the work. One other point is the increasing number of radio stations and television channels. As one can only "absorb" one programme at a time, there is likely to be a number of programmes that an MP did not get the chance to hear or see.

Another usage of the "mediatek" is for all the Members of a Standing Committee to be able to see a particular programme together. Finally, worth mentioning, is when a Member wishes to hear or see him– or herself after taking part in a discussion programme or being interviewed on a certain issue. Let me also mention that MPs may request in advance a copy of a programme which would not otherwise be recorded.

The list of programmes recorded is continuously under review to make sure that new and interesting programmes are included in the recordings offered by the library.

For the Library of the Norwegian Parliament to be able to offer this service, a special agreement has been reached with the Norwegian Broadcasting Company. This agreement involves no financial compensation on the part of the Norwegian Parliament, but the service is for Members of Parliament only and exclusively for use in the parliament building.

11.04 News indexing

Leaving the traditional and most commonly used media, I now turn to news indexing, printed as well as electronic databases, in other words, to sources handled more often by professional information workers than by the parliamentarian himself. News indexing may of course cover national as well as international news and events, but they are without doubt the most useful – and sometimes perhaps the only – means for news at the international level. As indicated initially, news indexing can be printed news summaries or databases. As for the printed news summaries they can be divided into three groups; firstly giving general international news, secondly focusing on events in one geographical area, while the third deals with one particular subject or organisation. When giving some examples of news summaries from these different groups, I will draw on the collection of the Library of the Norwegian Parliament. There may of course be other news summaries that are equally useful.

On example of a news summary giving general international news is the well known *Keesing's Record of World Events*, presenting itself as "a factual, objective reference source on current affairs". In the Library of the Norwegian Parliament Keesing's has been subscribed to since its foundation in 1931 and has been an important source of reference for international news. As it is now published monthly, and rather belatedly, it is no longer as useful for most recent events. Otherwise it is a valuable source of information on events worldwide. A similar publication is *Facts on File*, giving a thorough and reliable overview of events world wide. There will in most libraries by a choice between the two.

Another news summary with general information is *Wireless File* published by the United States Information Service (USIS). It gives an overview of political events written by various news correspondents. It is primarily concerned with conveying news to the American public, but will at the same time give information of general interest. As it is published daily, it is useful for the most recent events.

As for news summaries from various parts of the world, these are often acquired for areas other than the group of countries from which regular newspapers are received. They may cover one particular country or one region. In the Library of the Norwegian Parliament we have summaries covering one country or one region; examples of the latter include *Eastern Europe Newsletter, Africa Confidential* and *Latin American Weekly report.*

As for the group of news summaries covering a certain subject, or organisation, a parliamentary library will have to make a choice between a great variety. At the moment not too many are to be found in the Norwegian Parliament, not necessarily because we do not find them useful, but rather because we have not looked into what is actually available. Examples of what we are receiving are *Human rights newsletter* and *Amnesty International.* At the moment questions relating to the European Community is high on the political agenda in Norway. Consequently the library subscribes to *Europe Daily Bulletin,* which is heavily used. Examples of similar newsletters from organisations are *IMF Survey, EFTA Bulletin, ILO Information* and *GATT Newsletter.*

With the development of databases, and thereby the possibility of finding the latest news through such means, it will always be a matter of judgement – as well as, of course, of economy – whether to use databases or printed news summaries. I will try to point to some aspects concerning this matter. But before doing so, let me say a few words about the use of databases in mediating news and current events, again by drawing on the experience of the Library of the Norwegian Parliament.

Let me start by saying that the possibility of searching external databases in the Norwegian Parliament is fairly recent, and that such searching is, with few exceptions, entrusted to the library. There is today the possibility of searching in various news and current affairs databases. Some are national; like the indexes of two of the daily newspapers and the indexing provided by the Norwegian News Bureau. The latter will be the one with the fastest up-dating on news and events, but with rather short reports. In the Norwegian Parliament the party secretariats will have access to the News Bureau database as well, and will often, on a regular basis, supply MPs with printouts. Such printouts may be on subjects of particular interest or on the latest events, helping Members prepare comments which they are often asked to make on such events. As for the newspaper database, this will useful for "yesterday's news" and for commentaries, and access is for the library only. It is a full text database which means that a printout can readily be provided.

The indexes mentioned so far will, as they are produced nationally, give priority to news and events of particular interest to Norway. To be able to give more extensive information on international events and commentaries, the library will have to make use of foreign databases. In the Library of the Norwegian Parliament this means more specifically *Profile* and *Reuter Textline,* containing news and commentaries from a vast number of sources (newspapers, journals and news bureaux). These are full–text databases, and printouts can easily be produced and the library offers such printouts on various subjects on a regular basis.

The fact that Norway's relations with the European Community is high on the political agenda is reflected in the use of databases particularly the Norwegian *Norim–92* and various EC databases such as *Celex, Eurobases* and *Epoque.* These databases are very useful in helping the library provide the parliamentarians with the latest news in this field. Here too printouts are provided on a regular basis.

Having been given a priority right to search in external databases the Library of the Norwegian Parliament feels a certain responsibility, firstly to acquire the necessary skill and experience for the actual searching, and secondly to keep informed on the most relevant databases available. Finally the library also feels responsible for conveying to users the possibilities that searching in databases have for keeping one informed on events and political issues on the international agenda.

Before ending this part on news indexing, let me briefly point to some aspects regarding the use of printed news summaries as opposed to databases. Let me start by saying that each library will have to decide what is the better means; taking into account financial as well as professional aspects. What can be said in general, however, is that the use of databases tends to be more expensive than the use of printed newsletters. But then again databases give access to a large number of sources and thus a rather broad documentation. As for printed indexes, these are more limited, and the library will in most cases need to acquire a certain number from all the three groups mentioned above. While searching in databases requires a certain skill and thus is often left to specialist librarians, printed material is of course much more easily accessible.

The important aspect regarding databases is the fact that they tend to be more up-to-date than printed indexes and summaries. In most cases this is so, but the experience in our library is that this should not be taken for granted. News and events regarding the European Community can for instance be found just as fast in *Europe Daily Bulletin* as in EC databases.

11.05 Conclusion

To sum up then; there are no doubt many means through which the parliamentarian may be informed on news and public opinion. Considering the complexity of the new and more technical means, it seems fair to assume that very few Members, even if given access to databases, will do their own searching. It is therefore important to differentiate between what the parliamentarians are likely to do themselves and what is expected of the library.

For the MPs to keep informed on "today's news" and public opinion at least on the local and national level, this is easily accessed directly through newspapers and broadcasting. He will rarely need the assistance of the library at this point. When it comes to news and events on the international level, he may, however, want to use the library's collection of foreign newspapers.

As for his need for "yesterday's news" as it is defined here, that is including statements, commentaries and interviews made in relation to the news, he will, for all the three levels, rely heavily on the library; more precisely on the various forms of storage, indexing and recording available in the library's collection. This goes for information on public opinion, debate and discussions as well.

In performing its task, a parliamentary library may not only answer requests, but also provide information on current affairs and public debate and discussions on a regular basis directly to the representatives. This requires a fairly good knowledge of the fields of interest of various MPs, as well as of issues on the political agenda. It thus implies a challenge to the librarian, but as it also implies a closer contact with the daily life of the parliament it will in turn make a more meaningful job.

CHAPTER 12

INFORMATION TECHNOLOGY

Introduction

Irrespective of the size of a legislature, the need for its library to be able by promptly to provide relevant information to Members and legislative committees is imperative. For that reason, as well as the fact that space within a legislature's premises seems always to be at a premium, legislative libraries increasingly find it necessary to turn to the utilisation of modern technology for a variety of purposes. In times past, the cost and complexity of mounting and maintaining computer-based operations were fairly overwhelming for the average legislative library. With recent advances in technology and current competition in the world marketplace, that is no longer the case. In fact, computerisation has become a reasonably affordable alternative to the cumbersome, labour-intensive activities that characterise manually-based library and legislative information support services.

Chapter 12 of these Guidelines examines the primary issues that must be considered before launching into any computerisation programme, sets out the preliminary steps to be undertaken, and discusses the more critical aspects of mounting and maintaining computer systems. A basic glossary of computer terminology for the layperson is also included.

12.01 Technology Utilisation: Preliminary Considerations

In spite of the fact that computer usage is becoming ever more commonplace, and even though the relative costs of computerising various library and legislative functions has substantially decreased in recent years, the decision to embark on a computerisation programme is not one that any legislature can or should take lightly. While the potential advantages may be great, so are the pitfalls. Therefore, it behoves those engaged in the management decision–making process to consider carefully certain basic issues.

12.02 At the outset, two common myths should perhaps be dispelled. The first myth is that computers take the place of people and, hence, staff will lose their jobs if computers are acquired. Although it is true that computers can perform various kinds of routine tasks far more rapidly and efficiently than people, the utilisation of computers in library and other legislative information support work does not make the staff redundant. Rather, it frees them to apply their skills and energy to more critical and productive work.

The perception that people will lose their jobs if computers are installed is often a major stumbling block to an institution's making a successful transition to an automated working environment. The truth is that additional staff will very likely be needed to perform certain technical tasks with regard to the maintenance of the computer system itself, and existing staff will require specialised skills training to enable them to make effective use of the computer in their daily work. Such training, however, only serves to enhance their employability. In short, it can be said to be a job benefit rather than a liability for existing staff.

12.03 The second myth is that computers are not really needed in small legislatures or their libraries and that an investment in computers or related information management and reader services technology, therefore, is by definition unnecessarily expensive and frivolous. As the experience of many small libraries and other types of information–reliant organisations around the world amply demonstrates, this simply is not so.

Indeed, the size of either the legislature or the library is irrelevant.

In fact, it can be argued that it is considerably cheaper to begin an automation programme while the size of the library is modest, with respect to both its collections and services, and gradually to build up the computer system as the evolution of the library warrants, then it is to convert to an automated system when the collections are quite sizeable and the operations are concomitantly complex in nature.

12.04   It is crucial to realise, however, that use of high technology equipment is contingent upon the existence of certain basic conditions. First of all, the operation of such equipment requires a fairly stable and constant supply of electricity. Where there are chronic energy shortages, then, the use of computers in the legislature's library cannot be contemplated unless provision is made for a back-up electricity supply by means of a battery-powered generator. Even in countries that have a relatively high electricity generating capacity, power shortages do occasionally occur and, therefore, it is highly advisable to install UPS (uninterruptible power supply) units and voltage stabilisers to support computers and other specialised equipment.

12.05   Certain environmental conditions also pertain.   Computer, audio-visual and micrographic equipment can only function in areas that are free of dust, static electricity, insects and rodents and that remain within certain maximum and minimum ranges of temperature and humidity. This means that a room in which any such equipment is to be installed should be air conditioned, which will result in an increased level of energy consumption.

12.06   In addition to such human and technical concerns as those discussed above, investment in technology utilisation obviously entails serious consideration of the finances required, not only for procurement and installation of equipment but also for the maintenance of such systems once they are in place. Needless to say, the costs are real, and sufficient financial resources must be available to cover them. However, the affordability of technology utilisation must also be assessed in terms of the measurable benefits of improved workload management and higher staff productivity, together with the intangible but nonetheless desirable benefit to legislators of greater access to information.

12.07 Consideration ought also to be given at the outset as to whether or not the library should serve as the focal point for the development of an integrated legislative information management system that caters to the legislative support services of the legislature as a whole, or whether a system should be designed exclusively to meet the operational needs of the library. Arguments can be made in favour of both of these approaches, and many examples of both of them as well as other variations can be found among legislatures having functioning automated systems.

12.08 Of course, which approach is to be taken and specifically what library functions are either initially or ultimately to be automated, have a direct bearing on the financial implications. A single or "stand-alone" computer workstation, comprising a state-of-the-art microcomputer, letter-quality dot matrix printer and voltage stabiliser, costs as little as US$3,500 at 1992 market prices. Requiring nothing else in the way of technical support or renovations and operating on a very low level of energy consumption, it is easily within the reach of most legislatures to have at least one such workstation in the library and perhaps a few others elsewhere in the secretariat.

12.09 **Primary Steps to Computerisation**

Once the decision in principle has been taken to acquire a computer system, it is highly advisable as a first step to engage a qualified technical advisor to conduct computer literacy seminars for the senior managers and administrative personnel who will be dealing with matters of policy and finance, as well as for staff at the operations level. The seminars should be geared specifically to a legislature's potential use of computers. So as to avoid any possible conflict of interest, the advisor ought to be a neutral figure and not someone representing a firm that may ultimately bid for the project. An automation specialist from another legislature would be ideal for this task.

94

In addition to participating in such seminars, managers and staff should also make on-site visits to local computer vendors and to one or two legislatures which already have established computer systems. Such visits will enable them to see demonstrations of different equipment and to discuss details regarding other legislatures' experience with computerisation. This will aid in familiarising the individuals concerned with primary computer concepts and terminology, reducing some of the apprehension that may be felt by the uninitiated, while also facilitating the dialogue that will take place in due course with the computer technicians and sales people who will be involved at various stages.

As noted before (see 12.08), if the library is small and the legislature has no immediate requirement for other computer applications, it is fairly simple to a mount a computerised database for maintaining an on-line catalogue of books and periodical articles. From the on-line catalogue the library will be able to produce such things as topical bibliographies, accessions lists or registers, and charge records for books loaned out to Members or staff. Book ordering and periodical subscriptions maintenance are other library functions that lend themselves easily to a basic library computer system.

Where there is a high incidence of the failure of the electricity supply, then it is necessary also to maintain a traditional book catalogue as a back-up, so that manual searches can be performed during times when the electricity supply is down.

The printing of catalogue cards is another by-product that can be generated from an on-line catalogue. All that is required to mount such a system is an IBM-compatible microcomputer and any one of several commercially available, or "off-the shelf", library applications packages (otherwise known as "software"), along with a printer, UPS, and voltage stabiliser. Several of the smaller legislative libraries in Asia, for example, are maintaining such systems very successfully, utilising the CDS/ISIS software available from UNESCO.

12.11 If a decision has been taken to develop a library database as part of a computerised system to serve the larger information management needs of the legislature, the next step to be taken, after ensuring that all concerned have acquired some basic computer literacy, is to commission a technical feasibility and cost assessment study. Again, it is advisable to engage the services of a neutral technical expert, preferably one with experience in the computerisation of a legislature. The expert will need to work closely with appropriate staff so as to ensure that every aspect of existing procedures and related documentation are clearly understood for the purpose of considering different options for computerising them.

The feasibility study should set out the parameters for all of the various functions that could be automated, prioritising and correlating them as to their suitability for incorporation into an integrated system or their integrity as "stand-alone" applications. There are, for example, various administrative functions that can be accommodated in an office automation system or that can be computerised independently of one or another. Likewise, there are numerous legislative support activities that can be computerised together with the library database into an integrated legislative information management and "desk-top" publishing system. The latter, for instance might include transcribing, editing, indexing and printing all such documents produced by the legislature in the course of its work as debate proceedings, interpellations or questions, committee reports, and parliamentary journals; the tracking or Rulings of the Chair and of bills as they go through the procedural steps for the enactment of legislation; or producing other specialised documentation such as biographical directories of Members, chronological listings or histories of the activities and membership of legislative committees, and various topical briefing and background research papers.

It is advisable to incorporate into the feasibility study an examination of potential networking among workstations within the legislature as well as between the legislature and other co-operative partners, whether domestic or foreign. Thought should also be given to the networking of Members' Offices at the legislature and their constituency or district office. Even if the prospect may well be in the distant future, it is still important to do this sooner rather than later, so that relevant thought is given to compatibility factors which are critical to any networking possibility and, consequently, should be incorporated into the parameters for the systems design. This also will have to be taken into account with regard to projected costs .

In addition to assessing what should be automated and in what order, the feasibility study should examine the requirements for training existing staff, as well as the need to hire new staff having the requisite specialised technical skills to manage and enhance the computer system. It should also assess the costs of different options.

12.12 The technical feasibility study is essentially the systems analysis that comprises the basis for the next step in the computerisation effort: designing the system and devising the technical specifications to be used in the competitive process of procuring appropriate equipment, or "hardware", as well as the systems applications software.

While this phase is crucial to a successful computerisation programme, it entails highly technical work to be accomplished, again by expert(s) specially engaged for the purpose, with little if any involvement of the legislature's managers and staff, unless technical staff have already been hired by the legislature to take charge of the programme.

If the political leadership and senior management decide at the outset to make a sizeable investment in computerisation, the legislature would be well-advised to establish regular posts and recruit such people on to its staff very early on. However, doing so is not a prerequisite at this stage of the computerisation effort.

12.13 In countries where the computer industry is itself in a nascent stage of development and very few organisations have functional computerised information management and retrieval systems in place, there obviously will be little indigenous experience to draw upon. For these and other reasons, it is generally a good idea to proceed with a pilot project as the next step in the process.

Such a project entails the initial development of only one or two components of the systems design in order to gain requisite experience and, as may be necessary, to refine the design concept in the light of problems encountered under actual operating conditions. This reduces the possibility of scarce resources being wasted on any faulty or impractical specifications and facilities setting desirable systems performance benchmarks. It also helps ease administrators and staff into working in an automated environment and makes possible a gradual introduction of necessary changes in workload procedures as experience dictates.

12.14 The final step to be take in the preliminary phase of computerising a legislature or its library is the testing and evaluation of the systems component(s) developed during the pilot project. Systems testing and evaluation should take place after a reasonable period of experimental work with the pilot system has been accomplished. Usually a span of six to twelve months is sufficient for this purpose.

The database created during the pilot project should be put through a number of rigorous systems performance tests to determine whether the technical specifications have been fulfilled and whether the system is functioning optimally. It is critically important at this stage to assess any deficiencies and to identify any other potential weaknesses in the overall systems design, so that any basic flaws are corrected before other components are added to the system.

12.15 **Mounting and Maintaining Computer Systems**

Every government has procurement regulations to which the legislature must ordinarily adhere when ordering equipment for its computer system. Of equal importance to the procurement process are the technical specifications for the particular configuration of hardware and software that is required in fulfilment of the systems design. What can be a bit tricky is that some computer manufacturers produce systems that are "hardware–driven", while the systems from other manufacturers are "software–driven".

If a system is software–driven, it generally means that the software must be procured along with the hardware from the same manufacturer, and the tender must allow for this. In the case of hardware–driven systems, software usually has to be obtained separately from the hardware. This may be done by purchasing software "of–the–shelf" or by having it produced to order. If no suitable packages are commercially available, then the legislature will need to hire a qualified computer programmer or contract a software development firm to write the software in accordance with the technical specifications. Irrespective of whether commercial or client–tailored software must be procured, it will ordinarily require a separate tender from that for the hardware.

12.16 Mention was made earlier of the environmental conditions that must exist with respect to the installation of modern equipment (see 12.05). This entails not only keeping windows closed and ensuring that they are "air–tight", but also installing certain kinds of flooring and temperature and moisture controls. Beyond these considerations, installation of certain kinds of computer systems will require the use of special communications cables and may also necessitate the modifications of existing electrical wiring and outlets.

Making the necessary renovations in the area(s) where the computer equipment is to be installed is what the computer experts call "site preparation". Since it is a prerequisite for installing the equipment, the work should be initiated immediately after the order is placed and completed prior to the anticipated delivery date. Any technical requirements related to the site preparation should be elicited from the vendor when negotiating the procurement. Since the technical aspects of site preparation must adhere to the computer manufacturer's specifications, the vendor can usually be prevailed upon to provide any necessary advise or guidance while the work is in progress.

12.17 Assuming it was properly designed and tested, the degree of success or failure in mounting and maintaining a computer system will be a direct result of the skill and confidence of the staff who must utilise it in their daily work. Thus, the importance of giving adequate technical skills training to the affected staff cannot be overstated. In fact, it is only prudent to apply as much thought and care to this aspect as was brought to bear on technical matters throughout the planning and procurement process.

Training in how to operate the equipment is generally the responsibility of the vendor. To ensure this, the desired minimum training obligation, with regard to both the number of trainees and the total number of hours of training the vendor is expected to provide, should be specified in the procurement tender. Similar provisions should be made for training staff in how to use any software that is specially produced for the system.

Training on commercially produced software packages is somewhat more problematic. Many of the business that sell "off–the–shelf" software are retail distributors of a wide variety of consumer products and consequently do not employ computer software training specialists. In such case, staff will very likely need to be sent to a special training institute, or a qualified instructor may have to be engaged to conduct in–house courses for the library and legislative staff who will use the system.

12.18   In order for a computer system to be properly maintained, provision must be made for regular systems management. In those instances where the system comprises only one or two microcomputers, routine database maintenance usually can be performed by the staff trained to operate it. Periodic servicing of the equipment ordinarily will be handled by the vendor, initially under the terms of the warranty and subsequently in accordance with a maintenance contract.

Where computer operations encompass equipment installations at different places, or "workstations", and utilise various database applications software, it is highly advisable to hire a qualified systems manager. In fact, it is imperative to do so if an interactive system is to be installed. An interactive system is one in which several microcomputers are linked to one another by communications cables in a local area network (LAN) or where the system runs on a minicomputer or mainframe with a number of terminals spanning different organisational units connected to it. The systems manager will look after the equipment and database maintenance on a day–to–day basis, controlling access to the system in order to sustain its integrity, trouble–

shooting technical and operational problems, and liaising with the vendor. This individual should also serve as the principal advisor to senior management on technical issues related to current computer–based operations as well as the institution's mid– and long–term technology utilisation goals and programmes.

12.19   Similarly, to support the more complex operations mentioned above, it is necessary to hire a few more technical personnel as regular staff to work under the supervision of the systems manager. There should be at least one systems analyst and one or two computer programmers. Depending on the complexity of the system, additional numbers of such staff may be required. Among other things, these people will be engaged in training staff on different databases and developing enhancements to database programmes as the system evolves.

12.20   Another critical task to be performed by the technical staffing unit is the preparation of documentation about the system. Easily understandable user and systems manuals are required so that all concerned have ready access to necessary information about the system. Basic manuals describing the new system will be provided by the vendor at the time of its installation. If the software is to be specially developed, the firm or individual engaged to do so should be required to provide such documentation. Again, this requirement should be specified in the tender notice and contract.

Such manuals, however, more often than not are geared to a more technical audience and not specifically to novice users in a library or legislature. As further enhancements are made to the system, they also will need to be clearly explained to the users. An important companion to the more comprehensive user and systems manuals is a quick reference guide that provides brief step by step instructions for conducting information searches of the various databases. This is especially helpful to legislators and staff who are occasional users of the system. These types of documentation should be prepared by the technical staffing unit.

12.21 Networking

Earlier mention was made in passing to potential networking within the legislature and with other organisations (see 12.11). Unfortunately, this is an aspect of computerisation that is often ignored in the initial phase of introducing computers and other technology in a legislature, particularly so in small legislative libraries. In view of the facts that legislature's outreach is to a broad citizenry, whether national or provincial, and that the information needs of legislators span a broad array of subjects, this is a very short-sighted approach.

12.22 Even in a rather small systems configuration comprising at least two or more computer units, it is highly desirable for the workstations to have the capacity of functioning interactively. This is the basic concept of networking, and there is nothing very complicated or costly about it. As the network is extended among various branches of the secretariat, the system will of course become more complex and somewhat more costly to mount. Once installed, however, it usually proves to be less costly to maintain because it increases the efficiency of affected operations and concomitantly raises the productivity of staff. Naturally, networking with other institutions at municipal, provincial, national regional and international levels adds successive layers of complexity and expense but with a trade-off of greater access to information.

12.23 While the state of telecommunications in some countries makes it as yet unrealistic for any experimentation to be done with networking outside the legislature or at least beyond the municipal level, it is nonetheless important to consider the possibilities for the future when conducting the feasibility study. Moreover, it is incumbent upon those responsible for developing the system to incorporate in the primary systems design the requisite technical protocols that will enable the legislature to participate in larger networks, once national infrastructural development allows. Indeed, it is something that the planners in the legislature and its library should insist upon from the very beginning.

GLOSSARY OF BASIC COMPUTER TECHNOLOGY

Listed below are terms commonly used by computer technicians and marketing representatives of computer firms. They are defined in non–technical language for ease of reference by those managers and staff of legislatures, who have had no computer science education or specialised training in computer usage but who must participate knowledgeably in discussions with technically qualified experts engaged to design and install a computer system in the legislature.

Applications Software: A set of instructions in machine–readable form that tells the computer how to do a particular applied task, such as formatting a page of debate proceedings text or maintaining a catalogue of books in the Library.

Bits: Shorthand term for Binary Digits.

Binary Digits: The numbers 1 and 0 are used in combination with each other in computer languages to represent numerals and characters of the alphabets of the human languages.

Bytes: Units of 8 Bits, ie a string of eight 1's and 0's in difference sequences (10011001, 01110010, 01010101, etc).

Central Processing Unit: The part of the computer that lets it remember all of the information that is being stored in it and also allows it to do various things with that information.

CPU: Acronym for Central Processing Unit.

Consumables: Such things as computer paper or catalog card stock, ribbons or toner for the printers, floppy diskettes, and the like that get used up, or "consumed", on a day–to–day basis and have to be regularly and frequently replaced.

Data Processing Software: The applications software that allows a computer to search for and relate information stored in its memory and to manipulate the retrieved data in some prescribed manner.

Disk Drive: The compartment in a computer that accepts or holds a floppy or hard disk and causes it to function.

Disks/Diskettes: The part of a computer on which information, or data, is captured and/or stored.

External Disk Drive: An extra disk drive that can be attached to a computer to enlarge its memory or processing capacity.

Floppy Diskettes: Small, pliable objects, 3.5–inches or 5.25–inches square, on to which data produced on a microcomputer can be transferred for storage outside of the computer itself.

Generator: A machine that is able to produce a limited amount of electricity for a dedicated purpose or as a back–up supply in case of regular electrical power supply failures.

GigaByte: One billion (1,000,000,000) Bytes.

Hard Disk: A memory unit that is built into a microcomputer.

Hardware: All of the various pieces of computer equipment.

Input Device: Keyboards, optical scanners, and other devices used to put information into a computer.

Keyboard: The part of a computer, similar to a typewriter, that has several rows of letters, numbers, and command keys by means of which a user can type information into the computer's memory.

KiloByte: One thousand (1,000) Bytes.

LAN: Acronym for Local Area Network.

Laser Printer: A particular kind of computer printer that prints documents from a computer in high-quality type face by means of scanning the document in the computer's memory with a beam of light.

Local Area Network: A number of computers connected together with special communications cables that allow the computers to interact with each other, permitting the user of any one computer to access information stored in another computer on the network.

Mainframe: A computer that has a very large central processing unit with as many as several hundred peripherals connected to it and that has the capacity to handle very big jobs extremely quickly.

MegaByte: One million (1,000,000) Bytes.

Memory: That part of the central processing unit that allows a computer to remember the information that is temporarily entered and/or permanently stored in it.

Microcomputer: A small computer, often referred to as a "personal computer" because it can only be used by one person at a time. It can be placed on the top of a desk and, therefore, is also sometimes called a "desktop" computer. It can function as a "stand-alone" unit or as one of several work stations in a network. There are also small, portable microcomputers, called "laptops", that can be carried by hand and used literally on one's lap, and miniaturised laptops known as "notebooks", that weigh as little as 2.5kg and fit inside a standard briefcase.

Minicomputer: A medium-sized computer that can have several terminals, printers and other peripherals attached to it so that a number of computer users, performing different word processing and data processing jobs at the same time, can use a single central processing unit to store, manipulate, and transmit data in accordance with the instructions being given to it by the various computer users. As in the case of microcomputers, a number of minicomputers can be linked together in a "network" having a capacity equal to or greater than a mainframe computer system.

Monitor: Another name for a computer terminal, especially with reference to the one located near a minicomputer or mainframe and used by the system's computer operator.

Operating Software: A set of instructions in machine-readable form that tells a computer how to perform its primary functions.

Optical Scanner: A special kind of photocopier that makes an image of a page of text or a graphic display, such as a picture or chart; but instead of printing the image on a piece of paper, as a photocopier does, the optical scanner transfers the image directly to the computer's memory.

Output Device: Various kinds of printers and other devices that allow a computer user to get information out of the computer in printed form or to transmit information electronically from one computer to another or from a computer to a fax machine, and so on.

PC: Acronym for Personal Computer.

Peripherals: All pieces of computer hardware (terminals, keyboards, printers, external disk drives, etc) that are attached to a computer's central processing unit either directly or through cables and connectors.

Personal Computer; Another name for a microcomputer.

Printer: A device that transfers to paper, by means of some type of print wheel or light beam, information that has been produced on and/or stored in a computer.

Programming Language: A Special type of language created by computer experts for writing computer software. There are a number of programming languages just as there are many different human languages.

RAM: Acronym for Random Access Memory

Random Access Memory: The part of a computer's memory which is utilised while a person is producing a particular document or searching for some information that has been stored in the computer's permanent memory.

Software: A set of instructions that tells the computer how to do the job a computer user wants it to perform.

Supercomputer: A very large and extremely fast computer, used by some military and industrial organisations.

Terminal: The part of a computer that looks like a television and displays information on a screen; also known as Monitor.

Uninterruptible Power Supply: A piece of equipment having a built–in battery that supplies a limited amount of electricity to a computer system, or other electronic gear, when there is a sudden power outage from the regular electrical power supply.

UPS: Acronym for Uninterruptible Power Supply.

Voltage Stabiliser: A small piece of equipment that regulates the amount of voltage passing over an electrical cable.

Word Processing: The kind of applications software, comprising instructions in machine-readable form, that tells the computer how to create texts of documents, such as the proceedings of debates, bill drafts, committee reports, or correspondence.

CHAPTER 13

THE INDEXING OF A PARLIAMENT'S PAPERS AND PROCEEDINGS

13.01 Introduction

Responsibility for collecting, arranging, indexing and archiving the papers and proceedings of a legislature is often quite properly among the responsibilities of its library. Instant access to this material is wanted not only by the library and research staff who work for the Members, but also by Members themselves and by their personal staff whether secretaries, research assistants or constituency case workers. There is also a wider public for this information, namely, government departments, regional and local government, businesses, professional organisations, lobbyists and indeed members of the public all of whom may need access to the information which is created and published either by the legislature or for the legislature.

This chapter describes the system for the indexing of Parliament's papers and proceedings used at the House of Commons at Westminster. There are a number of reasons for looking at the situation in London.

First, it is over thirty-five years since an indexing system was devised and over a dozen years since it became a computer-based database known as POLIS [Parliamentary On-Line Information System]. It is therefore well tried.

Secondly, this system produces not only an online database but also, as a spin-off, the published indexes to all House of Commons debates and the published index to all House of Commons Bills and Papers together with the Government papers published for Parliament known as Command Papers.

Thirdly, the index system is available to outside users, on a subscription basis and overseas parliaments can also have access if they are interested.

Fourthly, plans are in hand to make the system available on a Parliamentary Network at Westminster should that be established.

Fifthly, thought is going into the use of a complementary full text system; POLIS itself is mostly a system of references to sources.

Sixthly, to the papers and proceedings of Parliament, there has been added since the mid-1980s, the other materials which arrive in the Library thus forming an integrated database of parliamentary, government and commercially-produced information. This paper however deals only with Parliament's papers and proceedings.

Finally, it is a system of some size as about one hundred thousand references a year are added and size, of course, causes its own problems. A description therefore touches on many points of general interest concerning the indexing of this material.

13.02 **The Parliamentary On-Line Information System (POLIS) at Westminster**

POLIS is a computer-based information retrieval system used by staff of both the House of Commons and the House of Lords and currently by a small number of Members and their personal staff. The database is, in the main, a database of references, not a full text database. It contains references to all domestic Parliamentary papers and proceedings and other material of interest to Members including official publications, selected European Communities (EC), international and foreign documents, together with the collections of the House of Commons Library. The system is managed by the House of Commons Library and largely created by Library staff. An office in the Department of the Clerk of the House of Commons maintains two of the POLIS database files to keep track of oral Parliamentary questions and motions tabled by Members of the House of Commons. In addition, the House of Lords Library indexes certain of its stock and research collections for inclusion in the system. Unless otherwise specified, this paper deals with proceedings in the House of Commons.

The main users of POLIS are staff at Westminster, particularly in the Library and Clerk's Department in the House of Commons, but also in the House of Lords Library and other departments of both Houses. This group of expert users searches the database either to answer a direct query from a Member, or as part of their information gathering when embarking on research on behalf of Members. Furthermore, a rapidly growing clientele is emerging among Members' personal staff, who can access POLIS from remote PCs or from dedicated terminals set up for their use in the Commons Library's reading rooms. Those Members who express an interest can be trained in POLIS retrieval, but experience has shown that the majority prefer to channel searches through the Library or their own research staff.

Responsibility for ensuring performance levels and running the technical aspects of the POLIS service rests with a commercial company which won the facilities management contract following an open competition. Such contracts normally run for 5-7 years, towards the end of which a new operational requirement is prepared and a new competition run. At present, POLIS is made available to users outside Parliament on a subscription basis, administered by the company running the main service contract. Government departments, the media, local government, and legal and consultancy firms constitute the largest proportion of outside users.

The current POLIS system utilises the BASIS text management system produced by Information Dimensions Limited, which offers a sophisticated and powerful means of searching the information in the database. Retrieval is possible on a variety of access points, for example – Members' names, subject indexing terms, dates, category of document, type of debate, personal or corporate authorship of papers etc. – or a combination of any of the above. For less frequent users who are unfamiliar with the command–based method of searching the database, a menu system is offered.

Queries to POLIS are mainly of two types: either to locate a particular item known to exist, or to produce a printout of all items on a particular subject, relating to a particular Member, or of a particular category of document. A substantial investment is made in employing indexing staff to analyse and subject index the material, in order that information can be easily and efficiently extracted from the database. The general proposition behind this substantial investment is that by taking care to index to high standards when information is first published, it is possible for staff subsequently to retrieve this information quickly and comprehensively when working for Members. This matches the tempo and style of Members' needs. Some 1 million records are now contained in POLIS, and the vast majority relate to UK Parliamentary papers and proceedings, which are indexed in depth. The Parliamentary material is split into different database files for ease of searching: (a) the PARL79 file containing records from the 1979 to 1983 Parliament; (b) the PARL83 file for the 1983 to 1987 Parliament; (c) the CURRENT file, which at present contains all records since the 1987 election. A new file, PARL87, will be created in the near future by extracting the relevant records from the 1987 to 1992 Parliament and the CURRENT file will then cover the Parliament beginning in 1992.

An example of a typical POLIS entry, a record for a written Parliamentary question (WPQ), is given below. Note that the full text of the question is provided, with the indexer adding helpful details from the answer and subject indexing terms.

[Field name]	[Data]	
ACCESSION NUMBER	440180682	[Unique identification number]
GROUP	PQ	[Document group – Parliamentary Questions]
TYPE	WPQ	[Specific document type within group]
DATE	18:01:93	
STATS INDICATOR	F	[Indicates reply contains useful statistics]
REFERENCE	217 c61W	[Volume of Hansard and column in the Volume]
SESSION	92/93	
CORPORATE AUTHOR	Scottish Office	[Government Department replying]

MEMBER	Banks,Tony; Monro,Hector [Member asking Question; Minister replying]
DESCRIPTION	If he will provide details of the current estimate of wildlife lost due to oil pollution in the Shetland Isles as a result of the MV `Braer' incident. – Includes table.
SUBJECT INDEX	Oil pollution; Wild animals; Birds; Sea pollution; Shipping accidents,sc [Taken from Thesaurus, see 13.05]
IDENTIFIERS	Shetland; MV Braer [Free indexing terms, see 13.05]

13.03 Parliamentary Papers and Proceedings

A descriptive account of the computer–based indexing system employed at Westminster will necessarily reflect the procedures and practices of the UK parliamentary process. The broad categories of Papers and Proceedings here described will, however, be familiar concepts in other legislatures.

i Business papers

Each sitting day in the House of Commons, a set of the House's working papers (the "Vote bundle") is produced, detailing the business transacted in the House of Commons Chamber. These papers cover the previous sitting day (the *Votes and Proceedings*), the order of business for the present day (the *Order Paper*), and items of future business (the *Notice Paper*). The Vote bundle also includes details of proceedings in Standing Committees and gives notice of Select Committee meetings (see point iv below). The House of Lords produces its own *Minutes of Proceedings* relating to the business of the Upper House. This one publication combines, broadly speaking, the information contained in the Commons Vote bundle.

In both Houses, the responsibility for producing business papers rests with procedural clerks, and the detail recorded is procedural in nature. The

Commons *Votes and Proceedings*, for example, records orders of the House, decisions taken, votes cast, papers and reports presented on the previous sitting day. In each House, it is the responsibility of the procedural clerks to compile a sessional *Journal* – the official published record of proceedings in each House. In the House of Commons, each Journal contains its own two–part index, compiled by the procedural clerks in the Journal Office. The first part is a straightforward alphabetical index of those papers formally presented to the House of Commons during the session. These papers include Statutory Instruments, reports and accounts of public bodies and other documents which the Government wishes to bring to the attention of the House. The second part of the index is more complex; it is procedural in basis. Proceedings may be indexed under more than one heading. Bills, for example receive their own entry in the index, recording the procedural stages through which they pass on the floor of the House. Other sections of the index pull together procedural material relating to all private and public bills. For ease of reference in locating precedents a decennial index extracts the more significant procedural events from the Journals covering each decade. Decennial indexes are published in separate volumes.

The Library's interest in Parliamentary working papers, however, is more than procedural; in order to fulfil its information service to Members it is interested in the content of papers, the subject of debates. While the POLIS indexers in the House of Commons Library work from the Commons Vote bundle and the Lords Minutes as important and early sources of information on the business of Parliament, they index other documents in greater detail, as outlined below.

ii   **Debates and Parliamentary Questions**

Each House publishes its own verbatim record of proceedings in the respective Chambers, including oral questions to Government Ministers. Together with answers to written questions submitted to the Government these proceedings are published as the *Official Report*, also known as "Hansard". An issue of

Hansard is published the morning following each sitting day and contains all the previous day's business, at least until 10.00 pm.

A team of indexers in the House of Commons Library, known as the POLIS Unit, analyses the Hansard of both Houses and creates a POLIS entry for each item of business, debate, oral question and written question. The entries for proceedings contain a brief description of the debate, order or motion; entries for questions contain the full text of the question and brief details of the answer. It is hoped to develop the system in the future to include the full text of answers as well. In both cases, significant effort is devoted to assigning subject indexing terms to the items. Ideally, Hansard is indexed on the day it is published, and input to the system the same or subsequent day. At a later stage, entries are also included for each Member's individual contribution to a debate. These entries are not subject indexed individually, but include a brief description of the relevant debate.

In a separate POLIS file, maintained by the Table Office in the Department of the Clerk of the House of Commons, a check is kept on the tabling (ie asking) of oral Parliamentary questions by Members. The system ensures that Members do not exceed their quota of questions awaiting answer at any one time, and it also generates a random order list of questions for answer at oral question time in the Commons Chamber.

The Table Office creates another database file, relating to Early Day Motions (EDMs). Early Day Motions are motions tabled by Members "for an early day". In fact, most are not debated in the House of Commons at all, but by tabling the motion and encouraging other Members to put their signatures to it, a Member can draw attention to a particular topic of concern. EDMs and their associated signatures are entered into POLIS and are printed in the daily *Notice Paper*. They are also subject indexed by POLIS Unit staff.

iii **Legislation**

All Bills introduced into the Westminster Parliament are indexed for POLIS in the Commons Library: public, private and hybrid bills; Government bills and those introduced by individual backbench Members. Each stage of a Bill in its passage through both Houses is detailed on POLIS. Proceedings are subject indexed, so that, for example, discussion of a particular clause at committee stage can be easily located. New printings of a Bill after amendment are noted, as is the final appearance of the Bill as an Act of Parliament.

POLIS contains records for Statutory Instruments, generally orders or regulations, which also carry the force of law. Statutory Instruments are known as "delegated" or "secondary" legislation, because the authority for making such orders is granted under a parent Act. All Statutory Instruments laid before the House are indexed. Those which are not so laid, mostly local orders, are not included.

Of increasing importance and interest at Westminster is the progress and effect of legislation emanating from the European Communities (EC). POLIS provides an integrated system of tracking EC legislation from the draft proposal stage, through discussion and adoption by the various EC bodies, to scrutiny at the Westminster Parliament and implementation in the United Kingdom.

iv **Committees**

There are two distinct types of Parliamentary Committees which have quite different tasks and which work in quite different ways. The papers and proceedings of both types are indexed for POLIS.

Standing Committees meet normally to debate a Bill, a Statutory Instrument, an EC document or a particular issue. Details of the deliberations of Standing Committees are noted in the daily Vote bundle, and verbatim proceedings and minutes are published some time later. There are also three House of Commons Standing Committees which may be set up to consider legislation and specified matters relating exclusively to Scotland, Northern Ireland or Wales.

Select Committees inquire into and produce reports on specified matters. They take evidence both written and oral, the latter normally in public, deliberate in private and then report to the relevant House. The report is published and so also is the formal oral evidence and much of the written evidence. Included among the Committees are a number of Domestic Committees concerned with running the House of Commons and sixteen Departmental Committees concerned with the expenditure, administration and policy of major government departments and their related public bodies. Evidence sessions due to take place each day are noted in the daily *Order Paper* and details of minutes of evidence and reports are recorded in the *Votes and Proceedings*. The House of Lords also has Select Committees covering the running of that House and quite an elaborate system of Committees on European Community matters. Details of their work are noted in their *Minutes of Proceedings*.

Select Committee papers are printed on the authority of the House of Commons or the House of Lords, and they join the set of papers numbered consecutively within a session as House of Commons (HC) Papers and House of Lords (HL) Papers respectively.

v **Reports and accounts to Parliament**

Other papers which need to be indexed include reports and accounts from public bodies, and various statistical publications, all of which are required to be laid before Parliament by specific provision in a particular Act of Parliament. They are therefore sometimes referred to as "Act Papers". On publication, these papers are listed in the *Votes and Proceedings* and copies are indexed for POLIS.

The Government will itself wish to present certain information to Parliament which it is not obliged to present by statute, and this it does by means of "Command Papers", that is – "at Her Majesty's command". Included in the Command Papers series are treaties, Government discussion documents ("Green Papers"), policy papers ("White Papers"), some responses to Select Committee reports, and reports from Royal Commissions and other committees set up outside Parliament to report to the Government on a specific issue. As with Act Papers, Command Papers are listed in the *Votes and Proceedings* when they are laid before the House of Commons. Some Government papers are laid not by command, but as a return to an order of the House; this is usually done to attract the legal protection afforded by the Parliamentary Papers Act 1840.

13.04   Published Indexes of Parliamentary Papers and Proceedings

The POLIS database is now well established and occupies a central position in the Commons Library's information services. It is, however, more than simply an online information source. As an adjunct to the online system, copy for two sets of printed indexes is generated from POLIS. These are (a) the indexes to the House of Commons *Official Report* (Hansard) and (b) the *Sessional Index to Parliamentary Papers*. Both the indexes are edited within the Library, and published by Her Majesty's Stationery Office (HMSO).

There are three different Hansard indexes: fortnightly indexes to the daily issues of Hansard which usually cover 10 sitting days; indexes to the bound volumes of Hansard (which cover the same period as their fortnightly index counterparts, but incorporate amendments, additions, deletions and other editorial changes to the text); and a sessional index, which is a cumulation of all volume indexes covering one Parliamentary session. A specially written program generates index headings from data in the POLIS records. Some headings are automatically generated and others are assigned by the indexers. Each index is arranged in one alphabetical sequence of Members' names and subject headings. Ministerial offices appear after Members' names where appropriate. Under each Member's name and under each title of legislation subheadings are arranged in two sequences: "Debates etc." and "Questions". Parliamentary questions are indexed under: (a) subject headings, (b) the name of the Member asking the question, and (c) the name of the Minister replying. Debates are indexed under: (a) broad subject headings, (b) titles of legislation, and (c) the names of all the Members and Ministers taking part. Certain types of business, e.g. ministerial statements, opposition day debates, estimates day debates, etc. are also indexed under those respective headings. Rulings and statements by the Speaker and her deputies are indexed under: (a) the heading "Speakers rulings and statements", and (b) subject headings. After a certain amount of editing the indexes are sent to HMSO in electronic format for typesetting and printing.

The *Sessional Index to Parliamentary Papers* is produced in a similar fashion from POLIS records relating to the three series of Commons Parliamentary Papers: House of Commons Papers, House of Commons Bills and Command Papers. These Papers include the various categories described under paragraphs iii–vi above. Index headings are created from: (a) titles of legislation and reports etc., (b) corporate authors, and (c) subjects. The Sessional Index is itself a House of Commons Paper. A decennial cumulation is also produced, although none has yet been generated from POLIS.

13.05 Thesaurus Control

In preparation for the introduction of the computer based indexing system more than 13 years ago, the House of Commons Library employed a consultant to prepare a subject thesaurus, a controlled indexing language, for use with the system. The vocabulary was drawn from the Library's existing manual indexes and from other published thesauri. Over the years the thesaurus has been refined, and considerable

119

effort is invested in keeping it up to date. With Parliament interesting itself in a wide range of subjects, and bearing in mind the richness of natural language, a controlled indexing language is considered essential in order to facilitate accurate and efficient retrieval. Users and indexers are guided to appropriate indexing terms, and they can browse around terms looking for related topics. Synonyms and acronyms are switched to one preferred indexing term, and standard thesaurus relationships are used to indicate broader, narrower and related terms. Scope notes are appended as appropriate to explain the usage of a term.

The POLIS thesaurus is, in fact, compiled from several subthesauri controlling variously: subject terms (concepts), identifiers (free indexing terms for specific entities, schemes, places etc.), names of organisations (including companies and other corporate bodies), names of Members and Peers, names of Members of the European Parliament, names of other individuals, and EC document numbers. By setting up validation checks against the thesaurus as part of the data input process, strict control over the data can be maintained and typing/spelling/indexing errors trapped.

13.06 Staffing

The POLIS Unit consists of 12 indexers, 9 half–time secretarial staff, one clerical officer, three staff working on the printed indexes, one Training Officer and the Head of the Unit. The indexers, who are university graduates with additional librarianship/information science qualifications, analyse and index the Parliamentary material and book stock. The number and quality of indexing staff required for creating and maintaining such a large database should not be underestimated. The training of indexers, given regular staff turnover, creates a substantial workload in itself.

The secretarial staff input POLIS material at visual display units (VDUs). While the indexers input a small proportion of their indexing work themselves with the aid of special programs, it is the secretaries who enter most of the POLIS data on to the system. The indexers pass work to them in a variety of formats: indexing forms, annotated pages from Hansard, marked–up printouts. As the secretaries' work is almost exclusively VDU based, it is a matter of policy, for health reasons, that the secretarial team are all part–time staff, working 18½ hours a week.

Proficient user training and support is vital to the success of any system. Retrieval training must be backed up with clear documentation – reference manuals, user aids, notification of new features etc. The POLIS Training Officer is fully occupied, and the demands on her time are ever–increasing.

The Head of the POLIS Unit organises the work of the Unit and arranges the training and development of the POLIS staff. Consultation with users is an ongoing and important activity, and much of the Head of the Unit's time is spent on planning developments and enhancements to the system. A large computer database is continually evolving. Indeed, it would seem that the more successfully POLIS meets the requirements of its users, the greater become their expectations and demands.

13.07 Conclusion

This detailed account of a mature computer–based indexing system for one Parliament's papers and proceedings differs from the other Chapters in *Guide for Legislative Libraries*. It is the only detailed description of a specific service offered to Members in a particular Parliament. But it does suggest, as mentioned in Chapter 2, that the legislature may represent an important part of a nation's information network and as such an important national asset. The indexing procedures covering both Parliamentary and to a degree Government information described in this Chapter explain the creation of roughly 100,000 index entries to documents published in 150–200 large volumes each session. POLIS is therefore a major project and although the procedures and publishing of other legislatures may well be simpler, (it is not necessarily an advantage to have a long established legislature), it is likely that all Parliaments will need to reflect and decide on the steps they need to take for the collecting, arranging and indexing of their own publications. And they should not forget the needs of the wider world whether it is the media which makes immediate demands, or civil servants needing to update administration or modify policy, or lawyers wishing to understand or interpret the law, or finally researchers seeking to put the record straight. Continuing access to the legislature's documents is vital.

A NOTE ON THE CONTRIBUTORS

Englefield, Dermot

Librarian, House of Commons 1991-93, Deputy Librarian 1976-91; Consultant Council of Europe [1970], N.Ireland Assembly [1972], Hong Kong Legislative Council [1988]; IFLA Parliamentary Libraries Section [Secretary 1981-85, Chairman 1985-89]; author of Parliament & Information [1981], Whitehall & Westminster [1985]; edited Commons Select Committees [1984] and Workings of Westminster [1991].

Floistad, Brit

Librarian, Stortingsbiblioteket 1990- ; Graduated from the Norwegian Library School 1965, worked as a librarian at New York State University Library 1966-68, Library of Norwegian Parliament 1970-77 and as researcher Fridtjof Nansen Institute 1980-90.

Heavner, Penelope Fay

Research and Information Analyst in the Office of the Director at the Congressional Research Service. Joined CRS in 1977 as a Reference Specialist in the Congressional Reference Division of CRS. Holds BA and MA degrees in Art History from the George Washington University and an MLS from the Catholic University of America.

Lindley, Jane Ann

Formerly employed in the US Library of Congress. Has resided in South Asia for the past seven years working with parliamentary libraries in the Asia/Pacific region as Asia Foundation and Regional Consultant for Legislative Institutional Development.

Robinson, William H

Deputy Director of the Congressional Research Service of the Library of Congress, having joined CRS in 1972 as Assistant Chief of the Education & Public Welfare Division. Currently is Secretary of the Parliamentary Libraries Section of the International Federation of Library Associations and Institutions [IFLA]; earned a BS degree in political science from Brigham Young University in 1959 and has a Master's degree in government and political economy from Harvard [1963].

Walker, Aileen

Head of the POLIS Unit, House of Commons Library.
Joined the House of Commons in 1982 and is currently involved in the planning and procurement of the third generation of POLIS [POLIS 3], which is due to be implemented in March 1994.